God Won't Save America

God
Won't Save
America

Psychosis of a Nation

George Walden

London

GIBSON SQUARE

Published for the first time in 2006 in the UK by

Gibson Square Books Ltd
47 Lonsdale Square
London N1 1EW
United Kingdom

Tel: +44 (0)20 7096 1100
Fax: +44 (0)20 7993 2214

info@gibsonsquare.com
www.gibsonsquare.com

ISBN 1-903933-79-X

CONTENTS

5

PREFACE

'Foreign countries are neither worse nor better than our own, only different.' So said my mother when I was going abroad for the first time, as a teenager, to stay with a French family. From a Scot who had never left our shores it was well-meant, generous-hearted and impractical advice. France seemed to me different from England in ways that were self-evidently better. The sun, the food and the easy *camaraderie* between girls and boys seemed to me a vast improvement on drizzly, rationed, sexually inhibited post-war England. After that I went every year. Smoking and drinking wine with girls in beach-side cafes at the age of sixteen while listening to Sidney Bechet's jazz saxophone on the juke box would have been illicit behaviour in England on all counts except Bechet. My conclusion about France's superiority in all things was later to be modified, but no doubt about it, this was a different place.

And so it remains. Countries have characteristics. To deny the existence of national traits would transform humanity into nerveless automata. It would also make it impossible to write this book. If everyone was pretty much the same no one would take much interest in foreign cultures, and America would be a nation without qualities, a featureless swarm of three hundred million human amoeba indistinguishable in their attitudes and habits from the Russians or the Chinese, in whose countries I have also lived. Like the individuals who compose them nations are a mixture of inheritances and influences whose precise mix eludes us, but which we have excellent reason to suppose are there.

Nothing, of course, is straightforward. The Chinese are an un-metaphysical people, while the French have a tendency towards abstraction. (André Gide once remarked on how the down-to-earth English *Stick No Bills* becomes *Défense d'Afficher*—it is forbidden to advertise—on French walls.) On the other hand no one has ever met an impractical, theoretically-minded Parisian concierge. And as the Russians discovered when they fell out with their Marxist-Leninist brothers in the early Sixties, un-metaphysical or not the Chinese made formidable communist theoreticians. Nor are a country's characteristics uniformly distributed. The lack of homogeneity in national temperaments is especially evident in a racially mixed society like America, not so much a cultural soup as a bubbling bouillabesse. Yet when all the encomiums to diversity are done and the contribution of each ingredient has been extolled, the fact remains that each national soup retains its distinct flavour.

The reason for spelling out these simple truths is simple itself. All I am saying is that there is such a thing as the American character, and that—with appropriate qualifications—generalizations can be made about it. America is currently examining its own identity as rarely before (notably in Samuel Huntington's book *Who are We?*), asking itself what it stands for and where it is going. At a time when it has become invidious to discuss whole societies without incurring accusations of arbitrariness, stereotyping and the rest, it is hard to see how useful answers can be reached. Fortunately people persist in putting the question.

To me it seems that a dual standard is at work. Generalizations about governments are allowed, normally of a negative nature, but to characterize the people who elect them is impermissible. Confining responsibility for the state of a society and its conduct abroad to governments is another way of avoiding the truth about national temperaments, but it won't do. If it were true The People would be absolved from all culpability (and denied all praise) for their country's behaviour. It makes no sense to treat grown-up people like children, playing down their faults and talking up their successes, to make them feel good about themselves. A character in a Martin Amis novel remarked that he couldn't understand how Mrs Thatcher became Prime Minister because no one he had ever met had voted for her. There can be a similar reluctance to face the fact that, like it or not, Americans indisputably voted (in 2004 at least) for George W. Bush to be their President. However you hedge it about this tells us something about the United States. The peculiarities of nations, good and bad, tend to reflect the temperaments and qualities of their peoples. As Plato remarked, where else would they have come from?

To point to differences in national temperaments is to make discriminations, which is to claim that one thing is not the same as another; a platitude perhaps, though even platitudes can be perilous. The latest edition of the Concise Oxford Dictionary defines 'discrimination' first and foremost as 'to make distinctions especially on grounds of race or colour', and to 'select for unfavourable treatment'. Only next are we told the basic meaning: 'to observe distinctions carefully, to have good judgment.' So it is that words can be subverted by current usage to the point where the primary becomes the secondary meaning, or is even turned on its head. To make discriminations no longer means to have good judgment, but its virtual opposite: to indulge in judgmentalism.

So it becomes invidious to say that Americans by and large are an energetic, liberty-loving people whose indi-vidualistic, entrepreneurial spirit has helped build a great and rich nation. To do so risks the implication that the Russians are a congenitally servile folk whose lives have been disfigured by serfdom and who, despite recent advances following the collapse of communism, are irre-deemably sunk in Oblomovian sloth, authoritarian nostalgia and collectivist inertia.

For the same reasons it becomes intolerable to suggest that the Latin countries of Continental Europe tend to have an enviably mature attitude to sex. Instantly the warning lights start blinking. For this might imply that, for all its surface liberalism and variegated lifestyles, America remains a country in thrall to Protestant inhibition, which might help to account for its obsession with erotica in all its forms and a pornographic industry with a turnover greater than any business in Europe. Reflections on American attitudes to business or on French attitudes to sex are only allowable if the Russians too are seen as paragons of entrepreneurial zeal and the Americans, like the French, are characterized by their carefree, spontaneous attitudes to sex.

There is one exception to the law of non-discrimination between nations, and to the rule that while governments can be attacked, The People are sacrosanct. This is that— providing it is negative—foreigners are allowed to say almost anything about America and the Americans. My own book contains criticism of America's religious traditions, its current government and its people. In today's atmosphere, where the war in Iraq has become a way of defining one's attitude to America and its culture, I should make it clear at the outset that, though an admirer of neither Bill Clinton nor George W. Bush, I am not hostile to the United States. I do not share the views of that growing band of commentators and intellectuals who appear to rejoice in every difficulty America faces, in the Middle East and elsewhere, and whose rancour has led them beyond legitimate criticism into some strange positions.

I have worked with American diplomats, notably during the Cold War, travelled extensively in the United States, spent a year at Harvard, and have a particular liking for American literature. In official and unofficial dealings, like others I have had my frustrations, though in general personal experience has made it hard for me to feel intuitively critical. American mistakes and miscalculations in world affairs tend to be large because she is a powerful country with vast responsibilities, and because her mindset, a product in large part of her religious inheritance, makes her less given to fudging than European powers. Talk of America's 'hegemonistic aspirations' leaves me sceptical too. Someone has to take the lead in world affairs, and if you dislike the idea that this should be America, you should see the others.

At this point I might be expected to describe myself as a 'friend of America' and my book as the kind of 'candid criticism' it is the privilege of a friend to offer. But describing oneself as a 'friend' of this or that people has always seemed to me a suspect stance; I doubt the objectivity of those who describe themselves as 'friends of Russia', of China, of Israel or the Palestinian people, or for that matter of Britain. The term is too cloying, too reductive, as if any intelligent person could feel uncritical friendship towards a billion plus Chinese or to three hundred million Americans and their institutions. I prefer to think of myself as not ill-disposed, an attitude which allows scope for franker criticism without being suspected of malice.

One point on which I confess to a measure of prejudice, if that is what it is taken to be, concerns religion. While retaining a respect for religious tradition—hence my interest in the Puritans—I myself am an agnostic. This of course makes me unhappy about what I call the pietizing of American politics. If the statistics about the percentage of Americans who are believers are right, that alone will alienate me from 80-90% of the population of the United States. But I have more confidence in the open-mindedness of the majority of Americans; so much so that I suspect that not a few of them, believers or otherwise, would share some or many of my misgivings about the dangers for their country of allowing their politics and society to become submerged in the murky waters of religiosity. If the evangelical movement gathers pace I am convinced it will damage their society and their international influence, to the benefit of people whose bona fides I distrust far more than I distrust America's.

A second confession: being an agnostic about religion helps to make me a particular sceptic about President George W. Bush. My fears about him increase every time I am told by right-wing intellectuals that it is a mistake to underrate his intelligence and ability. That is what Left-wing intellectuals used to say about the bone-headed trade-unionists who did so much harm when they were calling the shots in Britain in the 1970s. Nor are my fears about the mixing of politics and religion confined to the Christian Right. At the moment of writing conservative fundamentalists are the greater threat, but liberal churchmen appear to be joining battle. A struggle for America's soul between Right and Left-wing evangelicals is not a happy prospect.

Jefferson was on a wiser track. With his Enlightenment sensibility he had a dislike for literal readings of the Bible, but recognized that the country he was seeking to direct was a religious nation. A story has it that a friend once met him on a Sunday morning with a prayer book beneath his arm, and asked where he was going.

'To Church, Sir.'

'You are going to church, Mr Jefferson? But you don't believe a word of it.'

'Sir, no nation has ever yet existed or been governed without religion. Nor can be. The Christian religion is the best religion that has ever been given to man and I, as chief Magistrate of this nation, am bound to give it the sanction of my example. Good morning, Sir.'

That '*am bound to*' speaks volumes; what it means is that 'circumstances and decency constrain me', and the overtones of Johnsonian commonsense are comforting. It would be pleasant, if illusory, to think of President Bush responding in a similar manner. It was Jefferson who insisted on the separation of church and state in the constitution that is now in danger of being eroded, to no benefit to either and considerable risk to both.

INTRODUCTION

To say that America post 9/11 remains in a state of suppressed neurosis is one of those clichés whose only excuse is that it is true. Doubts about the future are deeper than at any time in the recent past, and as the Puritan leader John Cotton put it, 'From doubtings ariseth trouble of mind, and terror of conscience'.[1] It is a commonplace of psychiatrists that we shall never understand why we behave as we do until we go back to the origins of our predicament. The problem with applying their methods to entire nations is, where do you start? France and Germany, Britain and China have their national tics and phobias, but for them there is no clear-cut point to which we can look back to establish where it all began. It is part of her genuine exceptionalism that in America—leaving aside for the moment the history of native Americans—there is. We know to the year and the day when modern America's glories and tribulations began: the arrival of the

Mayflower three hundred and eighty five years ago, with its cargo of sturdy (if a little neurotic) spiritual mountaineers, intent on building their city on a hill. In that sense alone America is a suitable case for treatment.

To switch analogies: if you could X-ray today's America like a family portrait handed down from one generation to another, the image that would emerge would be indistinct. Some areas would be erased by time, others embellished by a later hand, and the whole would bear only a misty resemblance to the original. Though enough would be left to see that the portrait was executed by a powerful, decisive hand, and however much it had suffered from the interventions of time and man the outlines would remain intact. Beneath the haze of historical accretions a gray-white skeleton of Puritan bones would stare through. You can paint it over as much as you like, but it will always be there, indelible on the canvas. Whether you see it as a grisly reminder of times past, or the remains of an ancestor to be cherished and respected, is immaterial. Like the picture of Dorian Grey in Oscar Wilde's novel it will always re-emerge, if only because no nation can escape its past. And the less European America becomes the more clearly the Puritan bones show through.

It goes without saying that in such a diverse and complex society there can be no single explanations. Though this does not mean that all factors that have conditioned the American temperament are equal, and if we were to select the most powerful influence of the past on the present it must surely be her Puritan heritage. The route from roistering, multi-cultural America back to its narrow-minded, grim-faced Anglo-Saxon spiritual forefathers may seem long and circuitous, but no other strand in her history is so illuminating about America's current condition.

In one guise or another it accounts for many of the aspects of American exceptionalism that confound us to this day: why she keeps the death penalty long after the rest of the West has done away with it, why business is next to divinity, and why she is aberrantly obsessed with sex. It helps to explain why, alone in Western democracies, she has never experimented with socialism, why American workers work longer hours and have fewer holidays than their equivalents in other countries, and why she oscillates unnervingly between an isolationist and a missionary foreign policy. More obviously it is one of the reasons she finds herself in the throes of religious revival at a moment when secularism is advancing all over Europe. In other words America's Puritanical origins do much to explain why she is the maddening and exhilarating, ancient and modern, progressive and conservative, sophisticated and simplistic, creative and destructive country she is.

It may seem hazardous to generalize over-grandly about Puritan America at a time when the local store is run by Koreans and the garage by Latinos, and when some of the Wall Street operators currently jailed on account of their over-exuberant entrepreneurialism are of Slavic, Asian or Middle Eastern descent. Of course they are as American as anyone else, but it is possible to overstate the melting pot argument, both in regard to the amount of melting that has happened and to who has melted into whom. For all the dizzying mixture of races visible on America's big city streets it is worth remembering that to this day some 60% of Americans are Protestant and that one quarter are Protestant evangelicals.[2] In terms of religious affiliation they remain by far the most numerous group. Multi-racial America is a reality, but the ethos of a country does not change in mathematical relationship with its immigrant growth, and in its home country as abroad the contagiousness of the American way of life is legendary.

The idea that the origins of America's mindset are puritanical is of course hardly new. It was Alexis de Tocqueville's opinion that 'there is not an opinion, not a custom, not a law that the New England origin of American civilization does not explain.' In Harriet Beecher Stowe's *Old-Town Folks* Puritanism is presented by a character, at once sardonically and seriously, as 'the seed-bed of this great American republic and of all that is likely to become of it'. Indeed its influence on the American heritage appears so evident that it has tended to be discounted by sophisticated folk. The English historian A.J.P. Taylor ridiculed the whole idea of seeking the roots of American identity in New England. But then Taylor was a professional mischief-maker, and we can be sure that, were he alive today, he would be the first to discern Puritan echoes in the right-wing evangelical agenda.

More interestingly, the Puritan scholar Stephen Foster has advised against reducing Puritanism to a set of fixed characteristics and extending them throughout history.[3] That way, he warns, you can select any America you want. Clearly he is right: some characteristics of a culture can remain constant; others evolve with changing circumstance, sometimes beyond recognition. Yet such changes are more often than not intimately related to the culture that went before: the reaction against a Puritanical approach to sex in Britain and America is the most obvious example.

In any event American Puritanism is a case apart, if only for a single reason: that the evolution of its attitudes and beliefs has been crucially conditioned by their frequently self-conflicting nature. The biggest mistake that can be made about Puritanism is to regard it as a clear-cut, one-dimensional doctrine. Here is a way of thinking and feeling that is notoriously liable to double back on itself. Perhaps the best modern analogy is with the structure DNA—like Crick and Watson's double helix the Puritan molecule spirals around itself in a dizzying vortex of contradiction.

A fearsomely cantankerous system of thought, its chief disagreements were frequently with itself. It follows that there can be no question of establishing Puritanism's characteristics then following them through, laboriously, to give us the America we first thought of. The point is not to stretch them across four centuries to underpin an arbitrary idea of the country, but to trace their paradoxes and contortions with the aim of illuminating the America we have got.

If ever there was a case of creative tension it is America's development as a Puritanical nation. The Calvinist certainties the Puritans arrived with were fissile material, and from its earliest days America has inherited a culture of polarities. It is these base pairs of characteristics, embedded deep in America's warring soul, that have proved a source of phenomenal energy and of psychic mayhem. The fact that there are such different analyses of the Puritan experience is an illustration of this duality.

The arguments sway this way and that. The American Puritans were as bad as they have been painted, it is contended, namely a bunch of politically reactionary killjoys and control freaks. No they weren't, comes the rejoinder: a closer look at their daily lives shows that they were surprisingly human, and that the essence of their beliefs was not so much social control as individual freedom. Some say the Puritan experience was an aberration, an obscurantist interlude whose historical significance was submerged by the eighteenth century's shining lights. Others insist on its positive and productive features.

Debates like these, which touch on the soul of modern America as well as its politics, can excite Puritanical fervour on both sides of the argument. What often appears to be lacking is any sense that it is possible to be two things at once. The truth about Puritanism is that it was a schizoid condition, whose contradictions are becoming more visible and revealing in America today than at any time in its history.

It cannot be emphasized too strongly that the aim of this book is not to explain contemporary America uniquely in terms of its Puritan past. Rather it is to suggest links with that past, some of them unavoidably tortuous, which may nevertheless help to throw light on America's current condition. I am equally aware that focusing attention on American society then and now risks conflating some four hundred years. My excuse is that this short-circuiting of history may here and there ignite a spark of recognition of continuities that might otherwise be overlooked, but which to me seem relevant to the times.

1

PURITAN PURPOSE,
PURITAN PATHOLOGY

'They are traditionally exercised by religion, and adrift on the subject more than any other people on earth.'
George Santayana.[1]

Imagine an America with no *Mayflower*, and a United States minus New England. What kind of a country would the other settlers have produced?

Many of the earliest non-Puritan immigrants from the Old World had Puritan characteristics, so it would not have been unrecognizable. Yet today's America would be a different place, and not just in its religious traditions. The national temperament would be less earnest, less moralistic, less individualistic and on sexual matters less hypocritical. Some might think that an improvement on the America we have. But the country might also have been less energetic, less enterprising, less rigorously democratic, less uncompromisingly freedom-loving.

With no pushily self-righteous Puritans to show the way the upstart colonies might have been that much less resolute and persevering in asserting their liberty. The revolt would have flared eventually, but independence might at the very least have been delayed. The emancipation of the slaves would still have come about, though later than it did and by economic pressures, perhaps, rather than by civil war.

The WASP ethos would have been less potent and—just as important—the urge to reject its values less compelling. There could have been fewer Republican presidents. There would certainly have been fewer Bible literalists, and little fundamentalist revivalism. America would be less censorious about the sins of the flesh, but also less mesmerized by sex, and have fewer psychiatrists' couches. There would not be so many people in jail, and fewer—if any—would be executed for their crimes. One way and another America might have been a gentler place, less prone to the extremes of behavior to which a Puritan mindset can give rise.

Her foreign policy too might have been different, in ways that might appeal to liberals. But she might also have been less economically powerful, and so less able to do good, as well as harm, in the world. She would certainly have been more compromising, inclined perhaps to stay out of one or both world wars. And though she might have been more reluctant to become engaged in Vietnam she might equally have been less tenacious in her pursuit of the Cold War generally. Who knows, a non-Puritan America might have resulted in a longer-lived Soviet Union? And if a softer United States had vacillated over the Berlin blockade or the Cuban crisis the outcome might have been different.

The idea of a United States without its John Cotton and Increase Mather and all they represented for its future is one that might appeal to many Americans, nevertheless. For some time the fashion has been to play down the Puritan aspect of the national identity, as if America's early history were an affront to its image, and to later settlers. The claims of non-Protestant minorities to a role in the development of the American nation and personality are too obvious to insist on. Equally beyond contention is that it was the allure of the economic, political and personal freedoms of the Anglo-Protestant model, and the prosperity and stability they offered, that drew the majority of immigrants to America's shores in the first place.

Directly or indirectly her habits and opinions continue to be influenced and explained by her root religion. That is where the individualism, the work ethic, the legitimization of profit and the moral imperatives that have made America the most powerful and prosperous nation in the history of civilization come from. It is also the origin of the perception that America is a cussed, crankily religious, hypocritical, overbearing and generally obnoxious country. The fact is it that it is hard to imagine one without the other. The reason we can scarcely conceive of America without the Puritans is because it would involve dispensing with the ghost in the machine.

*

An historian once called Puritanism 'an admirable refuge from thought.'[2] By this he meant that the term tended to be bandied about loosely, largely in a negative sense. It is ironic that a word that was defined by its sixteenth century English detractors as 'precisionism'—in the sense of a niggling, carping correctness in the interpretation of religious texts and an endless judgmentalism about other people's behaviour—has become so imprecise itself. Few people today have a clear idea today of what Puritanism was; all they know is that they are against it. Somewhere along the historical line the word has changed meaning. Once a Puritan was a fighter for religious freedom, an opponent of oppressive monarchs and brutal bishops, a subversive in his way. A social as well as religious reformer, he may have been some humble cobbler or small tradesman who had pored over biblical texts after they were translated from the Latin and was tiresomely insisting on their literalness, along with his personal rights.

In the popular perception the positive, even heroic aspects of Puritanism have been forgotten. It is one of those concepts whose meaning has been narrowed and cheapened by careless use. 'Puritan' has become little more than a term of abuse, signifying a kill-joy and misery-guts favouring a drab conservatism in all things, especially sex. To the modern sensibility Puritans are quite simply a pain, the sort of people who, like the US Attorney General John Ashcroft, insist on the veiling of a nude statue, or on going to inordinate lengths to ban an allegedly obscene art exhibition, whose aesthetic nullity might otherwise have ensured that it never attracted attention. Alternatively they conjure the image of the least endearing type of businessman, whose characteristics include dutifulness, diligence, acquisitiveness, self-right-eousness, a stony heart, and sexual censoriousness, coupled with an inability to repress his own illicit desires.

However you define it Puritanism is liable to be condemned more or less in the terms used by H.L.Menken, who detested 'the whole Puritan scheme of things, with its gross and nauseating hypocrisies, its idiotic theologies, its moral obsessions.' In most people the very word Puritan is enough to evoke a grimace of Puritanical distaste. We are such an advance on them, the expression suggests, in our tolerant attitudes, our sexual freedom, our capacity to enjoy ourselves, the elastic breadth of our consciences. Frequently the grimace conceals a smile of satisfaction: 'Thank God we are not as they were' it seems to say. The irony is that in many respects we are more like them than we imagine, not least in their self-righteousness, but we shall come to that.

The Puritans' downbeat image is one of the reasons modernity tends to underrate their historical role and minimize their influence. What you don't like you don't spend time thinking about, and apart from endless replays of the witches of Salem in literary, theatrical of filmic form, interest in the New England of the time remains to a large extent academic. This readiness by many Americans to discount or disregard a large part of their own origins is seen as natural, yet it is surely strange. In few other countries do people disavow their ancestors so willingly. To the extent they are aware of them, the English take an instinctual pride in their early Kings, while the French have made a hugely successful cartoon series from *nos ancêtres les Gaullois*. The American Puritans underwent extraordinary adventures, but on grounds of apparel alone—those mournful capes and lugubrious women's dresses—it is hard to imagine a Puritan equivalent of *Asterix* in his fetching skins. Despite efforts by some historians to give them human attributes, the Puritans seem destined to remain perennially out of fashion.

One of the many paradoxes of Puritanism is that it is both a defining characteristic of America and a symbol of everything most Americans would prefer not to be. Like embarrassing elderly relatives the Puritans are an alien species who have somehow got entangled in the family genes: people you would gladly disown as having nothing to do with us if you could. Just as the modern English prefer to think of themselves as descendants of stylish, fancy-hatted Cavaliers rather than of hard-nosed, helmeted Roundheads, so there must be few Americans, even in New England, who would not secretly prefer to be the progeny of aristocratic southerners or of starry-eyed Pennsylvanians. Max Weber wrote in *The Protestant Ethic and the Spirit of Capitalism* that the Puritans represented the exact opposite to what is meant by the joys of living, and in the game where you imagine which personage from history you would most like to invite to dinner, Increase and Cotton Mather would be likely to score low.

*

Puritanism was the most vigorous form of Protestantism amongst the English-speaking people, and like many historical movements its roots go back earlier than we think: in England it began in the first years of the reign of Elizabeth I, and flourished through the Cromwellian period, before being forced underground at the restoration of the monarchy in 1660. It began as the faith of those who wished to 'purify' the religion of the Established Church from the taint of popery, and to insist on their liberty to worship separately. And it is 'liberty' that was to define its future.

The English Puritans were the indirect spiritual, intellectual and economic founders of the American nation, but the American version of Puritanism was radically different from theirs. The men who took ship to New England were the faith's most ardent believers, whose ideal society was a Utopia of piety rather than a model of class relations. Though relatively brief—the New England experiment was to tail away from the beginning of the eighteenth century—their reign outlasted that of the English Puritans, and their influence was to prove deeper and more tenacious.

Despite the Cromwellian interlude England was never a functioning theocracy. For not much short of a century New England was, and its beliefs were stark. Man is fallen and all earthly life is vanity. We stand trembling before God, naked and sinful, hoping for his grace. But (and here is the hard part) our prayers are of little use. Our fate has been decided in advance by Calvinist predestination, the harshest of the New Englanders' doctrines and the most alien-sounding to us today. The community of the elect they sought to construct was a kind of Darwinism of the spirit, with all the arbitrariness that Darwinism implies:

the fittest souls were predestined for salvation, while the faulty genes of the non-elect majority predestined them for hell. The criteria of 'fitness' were ill-defined, and nothing anyone could do would influence God's choice about who went one way and who the other. At first glance it appears to be a mystic creed, yet its logic was of iron. Because God's ways are inscrutable our puny human minds cannot anticipate his will: all we know is that for reasons beyond our understanding some receive grace, others not, and that is the end of it. So we get the doctrine of the elect and the rejected, the saved and the damned.

Outlandish as its theory seems, the idea of predestination is by no means foreign to the contemporary American psyche. 'A loser' is a very American term, as is 'a born loser', with its implication that society is divided into losers and winners from the start. Certainly America is sometimes presented as the land of the 'second chance', yet the discoveries of genetics, even though they suggest that individuals are predisposed rather than pre-programmed to behave in a certain way, seem likely to reinforce the notion of born losers and winners in the popular mind. We think of genetics as stark in its implications, but Calvinist predestination was starker, if only because the Puritans made no allowance for what we would call environmental factors in deciding who was to be damned.

The burden on the individual conscience could be crushing; introspection, a Puritan vice, made it worse. All the more reason to throw yourself whole-heartedly into the business of the world. For healthy, extrovert, talented and money-minded folk this most austere of creeds could offer tempting material rewards. The notion that the more successful you were the more you appeared like a member of the elect—providing of course that you did good works and prayed enough—proved a boon to commerce. In New England the prospect of getting into heaven became a business incentive. As Bible literalists, the Puritans could point to the parable about cultivating our vineyards, and the parable of the ten talents. As pragmatists they overlooked the story of Christ sweeping the traders from the temple, and the teaching that it was as easy for the rich man to get into heaven as for a camel to get through the needle's eye; with God's help a diligent and pious enough camel could, it appeared, squeeze through. That is what the merchants of Boston were taught to believe, and that is what America's more godly capitalists believe today.

At its most positive the genius of Puritanism was to reconcile God with Mammon, science with religion, and self-seeking with salvation. And like Republican presidents recommending the neo-liberal economic order to the former communist countries of Eastern Europe, or to the failed states of the Middle East, the Puritans were proud of what their doctrines achieved: 'The Protestant religion', in the words of Cotton Mather, 'hath not been set up scarce in any nation but it has made them, even in temporals, within a very little while, twice as rich and as great as they were before.'[3]

*

Debates amongst English Puritans anticipated many of the themes of the French revolution by a hundred or more years: hence what has been called the English Enlightenment of the seventeenth century. Politically and socially New England thinking was less progressive. The hectoring, polemical tone of their sermons showed that they saw life as an embattled state. Encamped in rugged, hostile territory, and with a Catholic King of England during some of their formative years, physically and politically they were in a state of siege. They may have been constructing a new Jerusalem, but that was the problem: it meant was there was no more recent model for them to build on. Theirs was a society that was literally making itself up as it went along.

Refractory colonials and fundamentalist churchmen, they were also de facto politicians and proto-statesmen, whose faith and zeal were to help set the moral and intellectual tone of the country for centuries to come. For these were impressive folk, and alongside their bigotry, censoriousness and hypocrisy can be placed extraordinary qualities of courage, conviction, industry, seriousmindedness, pragmatism and self-discipline. It was they who gave the American nation its feeling of apartness, its peculiar sense of destiny. If the negative had prevailed over the positive in their thinking and actions to the extent that contemporary prejudice suggests, the American Puritanical culture would never have achieved what it did. Nor would Puritanism have given rise to such outstanding figures as John Winthrop, the Cottons and the Mathers and—before he became a deist—Benjamin Franklin.

The difficulty is that whether in business or sex the history of Puritanism is rich in unintended consequences. Something in their system of thought ensured that, time and again, things got turned on their heads. Revivalists say they want America to revert to her spiritual origins and abandon her decadent ways. What they fail to understand is that, largely because of the doctrine of individualism inherent in the Puritan creed, one led to the other. American Protestantism was replete with internal conflicts from the beginning. Each belief opens the door to its opposite, and the cross-currents that result have tended to run to extremes. The Puritan 'dialectic' goes deeper than Marxist contradictions of class or economic interest, because it reaches beyond social organization into the mind and the soul. On the fringes of the Puritan mentality it is not too much to talk of a split personality, of Puritanism as a kind of psychic disorder.

The fractures and dislocations that resulted are there to be seen in the American spirit today. That is why America is more religious and more materialistic, more politically correct and more laissez faire, more moralistic and more ruthlessly capitalistic, more hedonistic and more repressed, more tolerant and more judgmental, more selfish and more generous, more introverted and more globally active than any other nation. The fact that the Puritan soul has dual attributes is one reason foreigners find it hard to size America up. Like the double image on a trick postcard the New England inheritance slips in and out of focus before our eyes.

One moment you see the benevolent image: of the successful, liberty-loving popular democracy and neo-liberal economic order that America calls on the world to emulate. The next you see a less inviting picture, which as an advertisement for the American way of life is the reverse of inspirational. The boom in pornography, the resurgence of capital punishment, the rigors of political correctness, the problems of overripe individualism, neo-isolationism, a corrosive guilt about the country's self-indulgence and chiliastic fears about where it may be heading.

*

'Its theory had been discipline' the English socialist R.H. Tawney wrote, 'its practical result was liberty.'[4] Liberty above all for the individual, who would be free to worship his chosen God and whom religion would free from his 'slavery to sin.' A moment's reflection reveals the productive and perverted effects that individualism has had on American life. Here was a source of immense creative energy—but also of angst, atomization and social selfishness.

Looking back at contemporary illustrations of those spectral figures in black, reading their finger-wagging sermons or recalling their ferociously regimented morality, the last thing that enters our minds is to think of them as individuals. Yet individualism was central to their creed. The Puritan stood face to face with God and accounted for himself through his conscience. The only legitimate authority was the Almighty, and relations with Him were personal and direct, rather than hierarchical and collective. Having responsibility for his own salvation gave him a right to think for himself—which became one of the reasons that Protestantism has been plagued by sects. Taken to extremes the primacy of the conscience could mean that every man was a church to himself, and sure enough, the Puritan poet John Milton once maintained that a church could consist of a single member.

The clash between self and society was there from the beginning. As a pragmatic Christian the Puritan recognized the need to live in a community, and this balance between freedom, personal choice and the needs of society was to be one of the underpinnings of democracy. Personal liberties had obvious limits, and the pressures to conform typical of Puritan societies were necessary because of God's moral law.

It is here that Puritanism has left its most indelible imprint on the psyche of the American people. For all the individual's liberty, in practical ways he was a prisoner of society. Or was. Today the balance between the individual and the rest has tipped the other way. Fragmentation of communities is occurring throughout the West, but in America the process is far more advanced. The Puritanism we think of as intolerably constricting in fact proved to be a harbinger of our religion of 'freedom of choice'. The prerogatives of the self over the collective—in the economy, in sex, in gun law or the environment—have today reached new extremes. That is one reason why it can be said that America is experiencing a crisis of the Puritan creed.

American economic dynamism is amongst the most obvious results of the Puritans' individualist economic doctrines. 'Look to yourself' and 'No man can save his brother' have proved a galvanizing creed, which animates and energizes America still today. The trouble is that the dogma of self-reliance is easily perverted into narrow self-interest, in which the needs of society take second place to personal greed. The same high-sounding principle of self-reliance could and does translate into a harshness towards the less fortunate; they too are left to look to themselves for their salvation, and to make out as best they can. Like contemporary capitalism Puritanism at its starkest could be a cold, unfeeling creed, whose social consequences could be bleak. In the modern age emphasis on the wealth-seeking individual can lead to the ghettoes of the rich, with Lazarus, 'the loser', awaiting his crumbs by the electronic gates.

The problem with personal accountability and the primacy of the individual conscience is that they can lead to a failure of that conscience when it comes to obligations towards others. America has a strong tradition of community help centred on its churches. But at federal or state level there is less of what Right-wingers would call welfarism, and Continental Europeans prefer to describe as social solidarity. For the same reasons high personal consumption, low taxes and inadequate public services tend to be characteristic of the Anglo-American economic culture. The downside of personal responsibility is not confined to the economic sphere; the sacrosanct aspirations of the individual can also conflict with his or her duties to the family group.

Seen this way it becomes less paradoxical that Puritanical America, with its idealization of family life (notably in *The Simpsons,* who always stick together in the end) suffers from the highest divorce level in the Western world. The constraints of marital bonds, like obligations to society, can stand in the way of the individual's duty to 'do their own thing' or 'make something of themselves'. The tensions are there in the vocabulary of family breakdown: partners running out on their commitments to each other or to their children often seek to justify themselves by saying they felt 'trapped', and in need of 'self-fulfilment.' Again we see how Puritan ideals can all too easily slip into their opposites: in this instance from the dutiful individual into anarchic selfhood.

We know from Puritan diaries that 'keeping conscience with yourself' meant submitting to a running mental check-up, adding or subtracting points for godly behaviour or its opposite, and generally measuring your progress in the world. A moralizing approach to your own life leads naturally to a judgmental attitude to society as a whole. The Puritan watched himself, but also other people. The result was a vigilant self-monitoring coupled with mutual surveillance, a fraught frame of mind which could result in nerviness and insecurity. To this day 'How am I doing?', addressed to the self or others, remains a very American question.

Nowadays this urge to self-improvement is as likely to involve perfection of the body as the soul, and the models for emulation more likely to be idols of the screen rather than the saintliest members of the community. When self-fulfilment shrinks to concern about whether you have the right shape, haircut, tan or muscles, perfection becomes a strictly non-spiritual affair. Consequently the characteristic reply to 'How am I doing?' becomes one that cannot have been very widespread in Puritan times: 'Relax, you're looking good.'

*

In many aspects of contemporary society—family breakups, drinking, drug-taking, corpulence, sexual promiscuity, immigration, low turnouts in elections, a collapse of traditional cultures—Americans and Europeans face parallel problems. In religion and its influence on politics they are going radically different ways. 'In America' writes Samuel Huntington, 'the yearning for rebirth involves a felt loss of identity.'[5] A rebirth means going back, but back to what? When the English dream of returning to a golden era it tends to be the pre-Puritan Elizabethan age. To them it seems the era of free-born Englishmen, untrammelled by inhibitions, a pre-industrial society which produced our greatest poet, a cultural and sexual arcadia. America has no such age to look back to, or to romanticize. The original position for them was the early seventeenth century, and whatever denominational guise it assumes, in one form or another the Puritanical ethos remains the most powerful religious impulse. America's God is a Puritan God, and in confused and contradictory ways that is what her preachers—and some of her politicians—appear to be edging back to.

No country is more modern in its material life than America and none more antiquarian in its spirit. European visitors are amazed at the prevalence of evangelism, not least on television. Individual Americans are too well-mannered to thrust their beliefs at foreigners, and many are not Christians of the church-going variety. Yet the knowledge that intelligent, educated, modern-minded folk may be privately convinced that there are angels in the air, or that the Devil is at work in human affairs, can be disorientating. In normal circumstances such beliefs might seem no more than quaint. Today they inspire wonderment mixed with apprehension.

Except to militant atheists, Bible reading or the holding of supernatural convictions should not be seen as aberrant behaviour. If they go out of their way to show respect for the Muslim faith, whose tenets and practices (notably on criminal law and the position of women) can be far more contentious than those of contemporary Christianity, how can sceptical Westerners be derisive about their own religious traditions, in this case the relatively innocuous matter of angels? But a majority of the world's Muslims live in poor, backward societies, and we make silent allowance for that. The US on the other hand is a rich, developed nation where the actions of the average citizen are not generally based on credulity or superstition. In commerce and the organization of daily life the same people who are on the watch for the traps and snares laid by the Devil are renowned for their supremely—even excessively—rationalistic behavior. As Michael Lind has written:

'When discussing politics, Americans use the language of Renaissance humanist republicanism; when discussing business, science and technology they are Cartesian rationalists; when discussing morals and religion, they tend to speak a Calvinist language of public confession and repentance.'[6]

Protestants of course see no difficulty in reconciling transcendental beliefs with the pursuance of their work in the world; for them one springs from, and complements, the other. Though now that America appears to be parading her beliefs for the world to see and admire it is hard to shake off a sense of shock. It is as if a friend of many years with whom you have laughed at off-colour jokes over a glass of whisky were to tell you that he is thinking of becoming a monk. Your reaction is likely to be that you have never really known him, and will never feel quite the same in his company. Above all you hope that, in the name of your friendship, he will keep his spiritual revival to himself. If only he would.

2

ECHOES OF NEW ENGLAND

'It was never merry world since there were so many Puritans, and such running to sermons as there is now.'
Job Throckmorton, 1589.

Arbitrary as they can be, first impressions matter, and since they can have no first impressions of themselves countries, like individuals, are obliged to rely for them on others. Before looking in detail at the influence of Puritanism on sex, commerce, politics and international affairs, it helps to glance around everyday America to see what strikes the eye as clear and immediate examples of the persistence of her Puritan ancestry.

Politically the most remarkable aspect of seventeenth century Massachusetts was the extent to which clericalism, clans and commerce interwove in the governance of the province. In that respect a satirist would have little difficulty in depicting contemporary American politics as a throwback to New England times. Now as then America enjoys godly government. As was the case nearly four hundred years ago its leader has experienced divine conversion and feels called upon by the Lord to rule. And as in those supposedly faraway times the President is drawn from a handful of ruling dynasties linked to business. Meanwhile simple citizens were and are officially enjoined to believe that the best hopes of salvation for themselves and their country lie in individual enterprise, in following the ways of the Bible and in frequent prayer.

Something of a caricature, perhaps, but then caricatures depend on an element of recognition, and excessive displays of piety by those in public office have always invited satire. The analogy can be taken further. The President's antecedents include some of the earliest Puritans. God-fearing folk with somewhat patrician attitudes, they had limited interest in questions of social reform. The first Governor of the Massachusetts Bay Colony was John Winthrop, a merchant, and New England was administered like some autocratically run family business. Liberty had it over equality, but liberty was subject to constraints, and Winthrop was an avowed enemy of what he called the 'democratical spirit'. Those worried by the rise of religious fundamentalism, and who fear that the terrorist threat is becoming a pretext for the erosion of human rights, will find uncomfortable parallels in some of the Governor's attitudes:

'If you will be satisfied to enjoy such civil and lawfull liberties, such as Christ allows you, then will you quietly and cheerfully submit unto that authority which is set over you, in all the administrations of it, for your good.'[1]

The contrasting backgrounds of the most recent presidential candidates, Bush and Kerry, are similarly evocative. Kerry's origins are more mixed than those of Bush, and include Jews from the Austro-Hungarian Empire on his father's side. And though he himself is a Protestant, the fact that he has troubled to see something of the world was enough for opponents to portray him during the election campaign as a rootless cosmopolitan, with particularly suspect links to the (Popish) French.

The most lurid proof of the persistence of Puritanical habits of mind in recent times was however when President Clinton fell from grace by the most common of human frailties, first through his alleged adultery prior to his election to the White House, then in the Monica Lewinsky affair. To the non-Protestant mind the entire procedure seemed surreal. Only America is capable of treating its president with solemnity and veneration, as the apotheosis of the democratic process, then openly discussing the distinguishing characteristics of the presidential penis. And only a niggling, lawyerly culture would oblige its President to debate, like Puritan divines quibbling over biblical interpretations, the varying methods of sexual congress. It is possible to claim that this extraordinary event proved the opposite: not how much this contemporary sexual inquisition reflected Puritan times, but how far America has strayed from her traditional reserve and how open she has become to uninhibited discussions of sex. Yet one argument does not exclude the other. The public pillorying of Clinton witnessed by an open-mouthed world was characteristic of the Puritan personality in one of its more warped manifestations. Like seventeenth century sermons against the sins of the flesh that could be designed to titillate as well as to admonish, the details of the affair were lovingly relayed in official reports and by a prurient media.

The way Clinton conducted his defence was similarly suggestive of the New England era. 'I did not have sex with that woman' is redolent both of Puritan logic-chopping and Puritan hypocrisy. And when the public concluded that in anyone else's language he had, in an episode that harked back to the self-glorying confessional tradition, the President paraded his partial *mea culpa* before leaders of the Church. The Puritans loved nothing so much as a sermon of redemption, and the sinner who atones for his crime publicly and with brio can emerge cleaner and purer than the man who never committed it in the first place.

The closest parallel Europe has to offer to the Lewinsky saga is the story of President Mitterrand's serial infidelities. In a Catholic country, where the right to privacy is enshrined in law and there is less appetite for the public airing of sexual misdemeanors, the facts surrounding Mitterrand's affairs went with him to the grave. (As the Anglo-American taste for sexual scrutiny begins to catch on even in France, details are now emerging.) It is a neat reflection of their respective Catholic and Protestant legacies that the French prefer regulation to liberalism in everything except carnal relations, while official America tends to champion individualism, personal choice and the free market in everything except sex.

*

Sensuality in all its forms arouses the vigilante in the Protestant psyche, and the simple acts of drinking and eating are no exceptions. The persistence over centuries of widely varying attitudes to the consumption of alcohol in different countries is remarkable. Here is a field where globalization has had surprisingly little effect on national habits. 'The abuse of drink is from Satan' the Puritan leader Increase Mather thundered, 'the wine is from God, but the drunkard is from the devil.'[2] Centuries later in Anglo-Protestant societies an atmosphere of sin and retribution continues to surround the act of drinking a glass of beer. While adult Londoners look for somewhere to buy it after the statutory eleven o'clock closure of bars (extensions have recently become easier), and adult Americans skulk about with bottles wrapped in brown paper bags, Parisians, Italians and Spanish sip their drinks in late night pavement cafes till the proprietor decides it's time for bed. And because taxes on alcohol are less punitive in Latin countries, the drink is cheaper.

Prohibition is perhaps the most radical piece of social legislation to have been implemented in any democratic country, and this too was a result of a clash of religious temperaments. It happened in the twentieth century, following pressure from the Anti-Saloon League set up in 1895, but the origins of the temperance movement went back to Protestant attempts to reassert discipline over drinking following the influx of Catholic migrants in the 1830s. The idea that such a swingeing law could ever have been enacted is astonishing; the fact that it endured for eighteen years, from 1920-1933, scarcely credible. When Prohibition was enacted France thought America had taken leave of its senses, a view encouraged by the fact that America was a prime market for French wine-growers. Instead of banning drink altogether—a wildly intemperate measure—American temperance crusaders might have done better to learn from Continental immigrants to drink wine with their meals in regular and moderate quantities. Noting that these immigrants suffered a relative lack of alcohol-related problems Andrew Barr, a historian of drinking habits, has written:

'But it has been an American tendency to regard the consumption of wine, like other alcoholic drinks, as a secretive vice rather than social conduct; to see drinking only in terms of the problems that have been associated with it, while ignoring its social value.'[3]

The trouble is that it was the social side of drinking that concerned the Puritans most. They were not teetotalers, any more than they advocated sexual continence in marriage. In moderation, they were in favour of alcoholic drink; it was just that drinking was justified on every possible ground except as a means to merriment. A glass of ale or cider with an evening meal was part of God's reward for a day's work well done, and the Bostonians were also great distillers of rum. Spirits were allowed as a means to warm the blood and for medicinal reasons (hence the sanctimonious name for rum: 'the Kill Devil'). 'Drink is in itself a good creature of God' said Increase Mather, moralizing in another vein, 'and is to be received with thankfulness.' A tot of rum was seen as good for 'invigorating the Animal Spirits, and brightening the mind, when tired with a close application to business.'[4]

It was the prospect of young men drinking and carousing in stews and taverns and all it might lead to that worried the authorities in the seventeenth century, just as it does in Anglo-American cultures today. There were problems of drunkenness amongst the lower classes, and incessant preaching against excess. In 1676 Increase Mather, who seemed unable to let the subject alone, caused a furor by claiming that visitors from the mother country said they had observed more drunkenness in New England in six months than they had seen in England all their lives. (The issue is now decided: the English, it seems, drink more.)

Outside Muslim countries, America—champion of individual freedom—remains a world leader in the regulation of alcohol. (Snatching a meal at Boston airport with his family, the author was amazed when his sixteen year old daughter was asked to display her passport when she ordered a fruit salad. The reason, we were politely but firmly informed, was that there might be a tincture of alcohol in the juice.) It is a striking thought that a six foot, eighteen year old male is adult enough to be sent abroad to fight and die for his country, while in most American states the same young man can be arrested for consuming a beer in the privacy of his home. The consequence of such draconian legislation is predictable: an immature attitude to alcohol reflected in a display of insouciance and competitive inebriation. In Anglo-Protestant countries the reaction against Puritanical attitudes to drink is taking a

similar course to that against sexual repression: a demon-
strative defiance of convention that quickly becomes a
convention in itself.

With the march of sexual equality the formerly male
prerogative of getting stinking drunk has spread to
women. (In countries like Russia, France and Italy by and
large women moderately drink.) From a libertarian
perspective there is no reason why women should not
drink as much as they can carry, but that is not what is
happening. Pressured by the gender war and by the
equation of alcohol with transgression, American (and
British) women have begun drinking, like men, in a taboo-
breaking manner.

In America (and in Britain even more) there is a type of
press photograph that cannot be seen anywhere else in the
world. An image so banal we scarcely register its significance, usually it consists of a young and attractive girl
sporting a glass of something and a cheeky grin. The
photograph relies for its impact on the image of a sexy
young woman, thrillingly courting sin. In a country where
70% of people believe in Beelzebub it is perhaps
inevitable that sex and wine should enjoy a perverse
allure, and the message is that she is a dare-devil, in the
literal sense: an emancipated woman inviting damnation
by consuming an alcoholic beverage. To give the picture a
point the caption will usually allude, as if it were in any
way noteworthy, to her drink, often in heroic terms:
'Putting it down with the best of them', or some such.

To the puritanically-minded food can be yet another
source of illicit pleasure. Until recently American cooking
has not enjoyed much of a reputation. 'Thirty-two

religions and only one dish to eat' sighed Talleyrand after an enforced stay in the United States. A century or more later foreigners were still lamenting the plainness of the country's cuisine. Octavio Paz wrote in 1971 that in the wholesomeness (by which he meant tastelessness) of its food America, alone in the world, had managed to link hygiene and repression in its diet:

'The relationship between substance and flavors is direct: sauces that mask tastes, garnishes that entice the eye, condiments that confuse the taste buds are taboo...Yankee food, impregnated with Puritanism, is based on taboo...American food shuns spices as is shuns the devil...Pleasure is a notion (a sensation) absent from traditional Yankee cuisine.'[5]

Things have certainly improved—to the point where the complaint about American cuisine is now frequently the opposite: in many American restaurants there are now as many exotic seasonings and outlandish flavours as sexual positions in the Kinsey Report. Even in modest diners, not to speak of the fancier restaurants that have sprung up since Paz wrote his essay, evading a superabundance of spices and sauces drowning every dish is the discriminating diner's most difficult task. Waiters who recite their bill of fare like a proudly learnt catechism can be disappointed to have their exotic offerings rejected. The explanation of what has happened is clear. American food has been earnestly eroticized, the insurrection against traditional values of plainness and wholesomeness horribly overblown. A crazed exuberance has replaced a sober simplicity, but a pietistic spirit pervades both, and it can be hard to decide which is worse.

49

*

'Topmost evanescent froth.'[6] Such was the verdict of the Calvinistic Scot Thomas Carlyle on clothes and fashion, another field where Puritan values, together with an over-strenuous reaction against them, continue to prevail. New Englanders were as neurotic about appearance as about everything else. Hair is a key stylistic factor in many cultures, and for the Puritans it was something of an obsession. Then as now hairstyles had a curious capacity to evoke vituperative reactions. The origin of the word 'roundhead' was hair cut neatly around the ears; any longer and men of virtue were likely to grow furious and call you names like 'shag-pole sodomite with hair like women'. In America such extravagant reactions can still typify the attitude of the red-neck moralist, even if his vocabulary of invective is less extensive.

Fashions change, and in a country where hairstyles can take on the nature of social and political statements, reactions and counter-reactions can proliferate with bewildering speed. After the 'shag-pole' look favoured by the Beatles and their American progeny, the Protestant hair-style has become inverted. Far from suggesting a return to purity, a close-cropped, 'roundhead' cut like that favoured by the rapper Eminem, is today seen by conservatives as an infallible token of degeneracy.

In cosmetics fashions have been less fickle. 'A painted face' intoned Cotton Mather in 1692, 'is a sign hung out for advice to Strangers that they shall find entertainment there.'[7] This time his warning seems to have stuck: in

America you still come across more women *au naturel* than in analogous countries, and outside the main conurbations the preoccupation with stylishness that has engulfed Europe is less apparent. For all its wealth, sophistication and occasional indulgence in baroque excess, to this day the dress mode of America can generally be described as wholesome. True, the Puritans—who inveighed against wigs and hats—would not have approved of their progeny's penchant for shorts. But by maximizing their volume, devising a unisex version, and extending them to the knees and beyond, as the French have been heard to sigh, Americans have managed to make even shorts un-erotic.

The overall impression is one of decorous restraint. Far from being sexy or provocative fashion has become a uniform obediently worn by tens of millions of Americans, whose sobriety of design and un-sensual colors proclaim a pallid virtue. Products of shops like Gap are characterized by earth tones and an absence of adventurousness, but it is not only mass market styles that maintain this respectable reticence: Abercrombie and Fitch sell similarly sober apparel, at higher cost. So relentlessly sensible are these styles that Madonna and Sarah Jessica Parker of *Sex in the City* have recently been recruited to star in an advertising campaign, whose objective is clearly to give a touch of glamour to an otherwise un-sexy product. The idea is presumably that people will wear the same bland clothes but feel naughtier in them.

The taste for a worthy simplicity runs from the bottom to the top. Presidents are either sober-suited or in jeans, and their wives seem invariably dressed in primary colors trimmed with Puritan white. Excess of elegance is one sin of which the American political class (like the English) cannot be accused. A rule of thumb is that when Americans dress neatly and cleanly they tend to be very neat and very clean; and when they decide to be racily non-conformist they dress down dramatically, though in a clean kind of way: sloppy tea-shirt worn with deodorant, pure white trainers, brand new torn jeans.

And jeans are the key. As it happens there is nothing American about denim (it originated in Nîmes in south-western France; de Nîmes=denim), yet in native form it has come to reflect American Protestant values perfectly. Fanciful as it may seem to describe a pair of jeans as a god-fearing item of clothing, in their century and a half of history that is what they have become. Hard-wearing, economical, unostentatious, signifying plain living and honest toil, blue jeans remain the most outward and visible symbol of honest-to-God America.

But in a Protestant culture nothing remains itself for long, and in jeans as elsewhere the Puritan inversion of values holds good. Worn as a fashion accessory or from cultural affectation, by people who have never done a day's manual work in their lives and never intend to, jeans tell us even more. Now the coarse cotton cloth in regulation blue takes on a more dubious symbolism. What it proclaims are equality and respect for physical labour, in a civilization where these virtues are increasingly absent. The bogusness of jeans, so ubiquitous it is no longer remarked on, is heightened by the simulation of a non-existent wear and tear: to give a phony impression of piteous poverty and endless toil they are stone-washed, mechanically faded, ragged-bottomed and (particularly when worn by mega-rich pop-stars of middle class origins), holed about the knees. Fake indigence, however, is coupled with erotic modelling. Unlike that of manual workers the tailoring of the more fashionable product is minutely calculated to emphasize each sex's primary characteristics. It is no surprise to learn that not a lot of the American jeans market, currently worth $11 billion dollars, is aimed at workers.

The wearing of stylized jeans could be seen as nostalgia for an egalitarian simplicity, were it not that the intention is so patently the opposite. The designer label on the back pocket, to ensure that the world knows how much they cost, and the mock humility of their distressing, makes them a perfect symbol of Puritan hypocrisy, culturally engrained. It was the ubiquity of jeans that made Andy Warhol single them out for praise, as 'something wonderful, something mass'. In his infatuation with the ordinary Warhol got things upside down. What he failed to see was that, worn as a fashion statement, blue jeans are the reverse of democratic. Instead they are the inverted, mass society equivalent of Marie Antoinette's rural affectations, as the middle classes condescend to find the dress of those perceived as their inferiors stylish or amusing. Another irony of the jeans culture is the time and money the stalwart American individual will devote to making him or herself look pretty much like everyone else. The fact that the jeans' manufacture may well be outsourced to poorly paid garment workers in China or Pakistan, then retailed at an exorbitant profit, does little to mitigate the ethical ambiguity of the would-be humble pair of jeans.

*

The problem about cataloguing puritanical attitudes or their inversion in contemporary American life is knowing where to stop. From extravagantly folksy politicians to an (often illusory) plainness in American arts and letters, the picture is the same. The modernist American tradition of flat-planed architecture, honest-to-God color-field painting, or Hemingway's terse, script-like novels are random examples. 'I can write it like Tolstoy and make the book seem larger, wiser, and all the rest of it' Hemingway wrote to Maxwell Perkins in 1940, 'But then I remember that was what I always skipped in Tolstoy.'[8] His view was shared by John Powers, a pioneering advertising executive active in the 1920s: 'Fine writing is not only intellectual, it is offensive.'[9] A cropped prose style, where even commas are seen as sinful, in that they signify convolutions of thought unbecoming to the writer of truth, is deemed virtuous, and Americans do it well. The inevitable reaction, from Henry James to Thomas Pynchon, can lead to extremes of decorative elaboration and a semi-willful obscurity.

In fact the Puritans' attitude to literary or oratorical style was as ambiguous as to everything else. Colorful rhetoric was allowed if the purpose was to arouse men to a sense of their worthlessness and an awareness of evil, or to denounce the devil and his ways. Otherwise an ornate style was sinful. To the godly mind, alert to sensuality in all its forms, even texts embroidered with references to the classics were seen as proof of carnal excess: 'So much Latine is so much flesh in a sermon.'[10] The didactic element in American writing is often strong, and the most surprising people could feel a desire to preach. 'I am too much a moralist at heart and really want to preach at people in some acceptable way rather than entertain them'[11] confessed the drunken and highly entertaining Scott Fitzgerald.

The antithesis of the moralist or plain man's writer is Nabokov, a dandified stylist and decadent European who became American by adoption. (He was as American as apple pie, he used to claim after moving to Switzerland, a remark whose self-cancelling nature lay in the home-spun choice of metaphor.) His major work, Lolita, written in the States but turned down by American publishers and first printed in Paris, could have been purposely created to offend the Puritan tradition. The one line in the book they would have approved was the remark by the anti-hero and pedophile Humbert Humbert, that you can always count on a murderer for a fancy prose style.

Another offence would have been Nabokov's sardonic tone. A sense of irony was not ordinarily a strong suit amongst the ministers of New England, though it is of course by no means the case that all Americans lack it, and the fact that this cliché continues to be mouthed by Englishmen who enjoy Seinfeld in their millions is ironic itself. Irony is nevertheless not a universal American attribute, tending to be more characteristic of Jewish than of Protestant humour. Literal-mindedness is a more general American quality, notably amongst religious con-servatives or the po-faced advocates of political correctness. For both of them life is an earnest business, and light-mindedness can offend: as a New York Times headline put it some years back: *Just Kidding, but At Who's Expense?*

*

If Puritan characteristics continue to exist, so must the characters they exemplify, and in ultra-modern America the visitor can frequently encounter what appear to be throw-backs to another age: the TV evangelist insisting in gospel-wielding language that abortion is the work of the devil; the businessman whose piety begins and finishes with morning prayers with his underpaid, overworked staff; or the devout feminist inveighing against the inexpugnable sins of the race of men. And amongst all the laxity and dissipation there still exist the truly religious, genuinely clean-living, ferociously hard-working and somewhat dour and disapproving middle-American type.

Though by no means all New Englanders four centuries back were Tartuffes, moral bullies, or morbidly pious folk. As historians of the period (notably Edmond S. Morgan) have reminded us, in Puritan communities at their most human there could be a certain sweetness. Self-control, steadiness of conduct, the avoidance of excess and consideration for others were Puritan ideals as well, and alongside the moral sticklers there were kindly, charitable souls, who knew how to amuse themselves. No doubt theirs was a sober mirth, but even that was an improvement on mirthless sobriety.

Today the type continues to exist in modern form:

plain-living men and women of faith who, far from being gloomy or censorious, can be infuriating in their equanimity, maddening in their moderation, and depressing in their indiscriminate good cheer. Brimming with wholesomeness they are liable to invite you to partake of a glass of home-made wine and maybe a little country music, all in an unspoken spirit of godliness. Conformism has its benign aspect, and insipidity, then as now, is a price we pay for virtue. (The type is satirized in the figure of Flanders in *The Simpsons*, a man of helpful inclinations and a celestial turn of mind who for a poor sinner like Homer turns out to be the neighbor from hell.)

A few rungs up the social ladder we find a more moneyed but not dissimilar type. Max Weber contrasted the blustering prelates and officials at the English trials of Puritan martyrs with the bearing of the accused, who displayed 'that respect for quiet self-control which still distinguishes the best type of English or American gentleman today.'[12] He was writing in the 1930s, yet in a certain kind of American we can still see what he meant. Visitors to the United States can be struck by the contrast between the persistence of old-world manners increasingly hard to find in the old world itself, and the brash, egalitarian style of much of the country. This stiff politeness, dutifulness, dignity and reserve are aspects of what Weber saw as the Puritan gentleman. Maybe it comes naturally, or perhaps it is something of an affectation. (The Puritans 'felt obliged to be civil to prove to themselves that they were sanctified' Andrew Delbanco has written[13].) Either way it is a reminder that if Puritanism was deeper and more tenacious in the United States than in Britain, it is not just its negative sides that have survived in *homo americanus*.

Amongst his most typical traits, everyone from de Tocqueville to the contemporary visitor has remarked, are his extrovert nature, can-do spirit and optimism. The country's wondrous economic, technological and artistic accomplishments are evidence enough of this. As a summation of the American character however this picture of an enviably active and positive-minded approach to life is incomplete. America's vitality is as elating as it is brittle. Her productivity may be a multiple of the world average, but she also has five times as many psychiatrists per 1,000 of population as anyone else. The deeper one looks into the dark side of the Puritan mind the more one recognizes its legacy today.

If faith is a consolation religious absolutism ought to be an even greater comfort, in that it provides answers to all questions and an unfailing guide to life. Nietzsche, for one, didn't think so: 'It is not doubt, it is certainty that makes mad.'[14] The Puritans were not short of certainties, or of the mental strains they could induce. Theirs was a demanding credo, and New Englanders could be a spiritually stressed-out people. The task of self-improvement began with self-knowledge, which meant self-analysis, and for all his efforts to project an image of calmness and self-control the Puritan was frequently a worried man. These were restless, ruminative folk, for whom failure or success, salvation or damnation, were not theory but stark reality. The consequences for mental equilibrium were predictable, and the American culture of the couch pre-dates Freud by several centuries. The difference is that in New England, though clerics sometimes acted as 'soul physicians', each man was a psychiatrist to himself, and mental therapy a DIY affair.

Today Americans wear their anguish where they wear their consciences, which is to say on their sleeves. To say that they are more likely than the citizens of other developed countries to suffer from anxiety disorders is nothing new; it is the figures that are extraordinary. The National Institute of Mental Health estimates that more than 13% of Americans between 18 and 54 are victims, and one in five suffers from a diagnosable mental disorder.[15] The American taste for introspection may have originated in Puritan angst, yet like many a Protestant trait the culture of anxiety appears to have infected much of the country: even the (Catholic) mafia boss in *The Sopranos* has his analysis sessions.

The Puritans were wonderfully resourceful but also perilously intense people. To leave a man alone before his God, with no intermediaries save his conscience, was the harshest of mental disciplines, and the result could be an inner loneliness. Christopher Hill has spoken of the Puritans' emotional instability, and Perry Miller concurs: 'The Puritan mind is one of the toughest the world has ever had to deal with.'[16] By this he meant the combination of physical and psychological strains their condition of economic and religious pioneers imposed on them. Along with this went the daily struggle between human desires and spiritual prohibitions. 'Chilling out' was not an option; the worst thing you could do in Puritan eyes was to drift through life aimlessly, in other words behave as the average man or woman is congenitally inclined to do, and take things as they come. (Dr Johnson, that supreme exemplar of human nature, had to force himself to work as hard as he did, and once confessed to a strong desire to do nothing.)

The mental cost of the Puritan drive for self-perfection could be awesome. The most routine aspects of life, from listening to bully-pulpit sermons exhorting them to recognize their sinful souls and repent while there was time to resisting the temptations of the Devil in bed or at dinner were a daily form of torment. 'Psychological vivisection' this relentless self-probing has been called[17] —a good description of the more gruelling forms of analysis in our own day. Work was a form of escape, but even that was just another means of attempting to prove their worth in God's eyes. And even when they succeeded in material terms, as their writings tell us, they knew all about feelings of emptiness and anxiety that can strike in the midst of plenty.

Taken to extremes Puritanism could drive you mad, and sometimes that is exactly what it did. John Winthrop told the sombre tale of a devout woman who, bound by her religion to confront her child with the sins of the world the moment it was able to understand, and uncertain as to whether it was amongst the few destined for salvation, drowned her infant so that it would escape damnation. The worst part of the story is that, like some classical tragedy, her action had a terrible logic.

Though responsible first and foremost for himself, a true Puritan was in danger of being crushed by an overwhelming sense of sin, the sheer hopelessness of living in a fallen world. So disabling were these torments that the clergy whose blood-curdling admonitions helped to instil such feelings of despair in the first place took to appealing to their congregations not to fall prey to 'dismal apprehensions about themselves.'[18] You do not need to be a psychiatrist to see that it makes no sense to fill your patient's mind with forebodings about eternal hellfire for the smallest lapse from grace, then tell them not to be downcast. Sex, of course, was high on their list of worries, and it is easy to imagine the frustrations of a society where intercourse outside marriage was banned by law, and where infractions were publicly punished.

Puritan doctrines themselves could be another source of trouble. Just as the theorizing behind today's psychiatry can addle an otherwise healthy mind, the creed could be convoluted in the extreme. Efforts to align their teachings with reality made Puritan divines masters of the subtlest distinctions, and the results could be perplexing to the congregation, as counter-commonsensical notions abounded in their writings and sermons. Sincerity, for example, may seem preferable to hypocrisy, yet to New England logic-choppers it could be the other way round. The advantage of hypocrisy, it was argued, was that it implied recognition that there was an ideal to which you should at least pretend to aspire. Lip service to good behaviour, even if you didn't carry it through in practice, could be counted as virtue of a sort. (H.L. Mencken, scourge of hypocrisy, was to put the same idea more sardonically when he wrote: 'A reputation for chastity is a fine and wonderful thing. Chastity itself is sometimes useful.'[19])

Sincerity, on the other hand, did not necessarily imply

purity of heart, since it can be used to excuse any conduct and sanctify any cause. (Hitler is the clearest contemporary example. His hatred of the Jews was unquestionably sincere, and since he made no secret of his feelings, and put them into practice, he was not a hypocrite.) Another thing that worried the Puritans about sincerity was that it sprang from the heart, rather than the mind. The sincere person can be imbued with the conviction that he or she has no further need to know or to learn: to say that you are sincere in your beliefs dispenses you from reflecting on what exactly it is you believe, and why. Excessive sincerity also carries the danger of indulging in gushings of warm, self-gratifying emotion. Self-righteous the Puritans often were, but rarely self-gratifying; they were too much addicted to psychological suffering for that.

*

Anxiety in modern America is as likely to take bodily as spiritual forms. What, for example, could be more redolent of Puritan angst than America's infatuation with the gym? How would a New England clergyman have reacted to the sight of a roomful of men and women sweating it out? The earnest, stoical atmosphere would attract him. Most of all he would be gratified by the spectacle of mass suffering in the expiation of the sins of sloth and self-indulgence, and pleased to discover that they felt cleansed after their bouts of self-chastisement, corporately born-again men and women. On the other hand he would be uncomfortable at the sight of so much male and female flesh, promiscuously mixed. The cult of carnal beauty, of leanness and fitness for their own sake, would also arouse suspicions: the striving for perfection, it might seem to him, had been transferred from soul to body. Ever-ready to see theological implications in daily behaviour, he might suspect that the modern version of predestination was that the Thin are the new Elect whereas the Fat shall sweat in hell.

The Puritans were keen on exercise, if only for martial reasons, but this was something else. The insistent beat of the music, with its suggestion of erotic pleasures— pleasures for which the body was being minutely tuned— would be another worry. Seemingly a place of expiation, the gym could be a preparatory course for sin. How much pain the addicts were prepared to endure for a few brief moments of pleasure! But then pleasure, he might conclude wistfully, was the new Protestant ethic: something to be worked at tirelessly, dutifully, relentlessly.

Overall, his verdict would be negative. The pointless-ness of the movements—the running nowhere, the lifting of weights to no purpose, the rowing of imaginary boats, the stretchings and bendings and limberings up—would be the clue to what was happening. What, in the end, did the gym represent? Vanity, in all senses of the word, and a final and complete submission to the carnal, material life. Whatever their religious professions twenty first century Americans, with their craving for everlasting youth and for staving off mortality, were clearly a people smitten by disbelief in the eternal life.

*

Protestantism is about protest, and protest infected by pietism quickly produces new types of conformity. Hence the tendency of Americans (and of the English) to pursue their rebellions against convention with an earnestness worthy of Puritan divines. In a tradition of constriction and repression the most natural behaviour, such as a relaxed and humane approach to the weaknesses of the flesh or the enjoyment of the sensual side of life, can take on the proportions of a rebellious act, a whole new way of living, invented not over several millennia of human existence but by twentieth-first century Americans.

In speaking of the pietism of the protester I am not thinking primarily of political dissent, though that is a part. Nor do I mean protest in its more obviously contrived and attention-seeking aspects ('obscene' art, hippy antics), which are merely the most visible external signs. What matters is the extent to which would-be antinomian attitudes have been institutionalized in daily life. To see how counter-cultural affectations have become America's daily bread we must look not to the young, where it has long been the noisy norm, but to the middle-aged, the well-heeled and in all respects respectable.

The personal ads placed by divorced women looking for replacement partners in up-market magazines tell us more about the American Puritan mindset in its pseudo-rebellious mode than the more eye-catching stunts of people forty years their junior. Jokily phrased as they often are, these are serious social documents: carefully drawn up prospectuses which combine a lifetime's knowledge and experience with a feeling that at many places along the line somehow they have missed out. The more carefree

the 'merry widow' tone of the ads the more clearly we
discern desperate souls aching to adapt. Naturalness is
supposedly the hallmark of the liberated modern self, yet
the determinedly emancipated style of these intimate self-
characterizations reeks of existential angst. Not a few of
those who present themselves as dissident souls, it is safe
to assume, are in the brittle psychological state of people
who are striving to convince themselves of things which
do not come naturally to them at all.

In previous eras a mature woman advertising herself
for re-marriage would make play with her faith,
respectability and obedience. Now she will make a virtue
of her independence, her absence of inhibition and wide-
openness to the sensual life. The last thing she will do is
to vaunt her religious feelings, if any, which does not
prevent her writing up her CV in an incantatory style
worthy of a godly widow. The dominant theme of these
ladies of matronly age are hints at the transgressive. The
following excerpts from real-life ads give the flavour:

> Dynamic and sexy widow... feminine, spiritual,
> adaptable, divorced... Never quite fit lawyer
> mold... too much of a sense of humour...
> spontaneous... cerebral discussions, dancing in the
> kitchen... passionate about art...fulfilled romantic
> adventures... sleeping under the stars and skinny-
> dipping early in the morning...wining, dining, fun,
> frolic... loves Pinot noir... devilish playfulness...
> loves Miles Davis.[20]

But for all this abandonment to nature and Dionysian

powers, first things first: in fine old-fashioned style at the end of the ad there is frequently a polite insistence that the lucky man must be 'financially comfortable.'

The most revealing thing about such ads is how these supposedly unconventional folk depict themselves in virtually identical terms. Each one presents herself as only a little short of hip, yet what emerges from this picture of wayward individualism is a single recognizable type. Indeed it is impossible to imagine a 50-60 year old woman setting out her stall in any other terms; a lady advertising herself as—'hates drink, drugs and Miles Davis…for chaste, intellectual companionship' would be an intriguingly off-beat creature. Another key to the decoding of these ads is their meticulousness, revealed in the carefully calibrated deviance from what the author touchingly imagines to be a repressive norm. The tentative nature of her insurrections underscores her essential primness.

In America the normalizing of transgression works at all levels of would-be unconventional conduct. How it is that what has long become routine behaviour can continue to succeed in projecting an off-beat image is a mystery of contemporary culture, for which the only explanations are social hypocrisy, the mythologies of commerce, and personal self-delusion.

*

From tragically merry widows to the sexually eccentric works of Robert Mapplethorpe may seem a long step, yet in different registers they are in similar lines of business. Both are marketing themselves as counter-cultural figures

(Mapplethorpe features himself in some of his photographs), and in each case a cash reward is part of the deal. The object of Mapplethorpe's work, like that of the divorcee's ad, is the glamorization of transgression, and a better instance of Puritanism inverted is difficult to imagine. Only in a culture where a taste for Pinot noir can be equated with a certain delicious decadence can the divorcee imagine she has anything distinctive to sell, and only a country where a majority of people believe in the reality of the devil can be indignant at Mapplethorpe's naked human bodies or (rather dated) satanic themes. Executed with technical refinement and (in the photographic sense) great good taste they fall squarely into the category of the taboo-breaking tradition.

Whether it is the skinny-dipping matron or Mapplethorpe's naked penises (one can well imagine our widow approving, with a little shudder of daring, the photographer's work) each relies on a lively sense of sin for their 'disturbing' effects. But at the center of it all a certain phoniness is at work. In the kind of society whose repressive instincts and dark obsessions Mapplethorpe's images are meant to play on, his photographs would be banned. The fact that they enjoyed mostly unhindered display and were openly praised by many critics, suggests that 'transgression', if not yet the norm, is well on the way to normalization. ('Cooptation' was Susan Sontag's word for the phenomenon.[21]) This undercuts their adversarial ethos and—technical skill aside—a good deal of their interest. What Mapplethorpe and artists like him need to validate their images is what religious fundamentalists would be only too happy to provide: a thoroughgoing censorship, backed by law. Sadly for the fundamentalists, as well as for the 'adversarial' artists, they are unlikely to get it.

In Puritan times enterprising individuals made a career for themselves in the church. The prospects were all the more attractive in that the clerical path was by no means incompatible, as John Winthrop had shown, with trade and commerce. Today people with a pietistic mindset, albeit of the liberal variety, trade in the counter-culture as in any other line of business. The reservoir of customers is vast and the rewards (eg in the film industry) can be colossal. The personal satisfactions can be considerable too: like the Puritans before them, they have little difficulty in convincing themselves of their claim to a monopoly of the high moral ground. During last year's G8 pop concerts directed at raising awareness of suffering in Africa, super-rich British and American rock stars who donated a day or two of their time were treated in the media as something little short of a community of saints.

An advantage enjoyed by American artists, writers and singers is that in the United States the remnants of a puritanical culture against which to give a plausible impersonation of rebelling continue to exist. (In Europe Bible literalists or advocates of sexual continence before marriage are thin on the ground.) Though the fact that the clash of values is more often something of a charade from which each side draws moral sustenance does little to diminish the attractions of the confrontation. Abortion, gay marriage, or the teaching of religion in schools can be genuinely contentious issues, but from there to a reactionary moral order dominating the entire culture is a long distance. America doesn't look like that, and it doesn't feel like that either.

In the arts and entertainment industries one might almost speak of a nostalgia for repression. Films like *American Beauty* and TV series like *Desperate Housewives* satisfy domestic and international audiences because they hold up a caricature of suburban American life for our delectation and derision. A reason for the success of *American Beauty* was that it made everyone feel good to smile at the regulation of family life it pictures: the formal meals at table to a background of classical music, and the adolescent dragged from her room to be placed between her bickering parents. An effective caricature must be essentially true, and this scenario isn't. In reality the moping daughter would take her meals where and when she wanted them, probably in her room watching TV, and the music that filled the silences over her parents' dinner table would have been slightly dated pop.

The trouble is, no one would have smiled at that. Echoes of a Puritanical family life are essential to the enterprise. Without them there could be no exposure of the husband's hypocrisy when he becomes besotted with his daughter's girlfriend, or revelation that the quiet suburban setting is in fact a sump of sin and fornication, of drugs, adultery, homosexuality, and fascistic Vietnam veterans. The essence of the plot of the TV serial *Desperate Housewives* is virtually identical: outer respectability, inner mayhem.

If we take the divorcees' ads, the photos of genitalia naked and aroused, and the screen images of America at face value, we get a country where wine is a daring indulgence, family conventions much as they were in the Fifties, and artists are driven to extreme gestures of revolt against stifling and hypocritical convention. Of course there is no lack of people, notably on the Christian Right, who might be happy to make this fantasy America a reality, but for the moment fantasy it remains. It is one with a curiously make-believe aspect, 'as if' vast swathes of America were to this day a fully functioning New England society, whose repressive instincts scandalize decent, progressive folk and thereby validate protest and rebellion.

The reason that almost nothing changes as a consequence of these supposedly subversive products of the cinema or art is because the change has already occurred, predominantly in the Sixties. Yet almost half a century later the Puritan dialectic of repression and revolt continues, as a kind of shadow-boxing. That is the new convention and everyone—audiences included—is in on the game. TV producers, artists or film-makers go on 'exposing' the selfsame vanities, venality and hypocrisies of suburban or small town America they exposed the year before, and the year before that, and it is a safe bet that they will do it again in years to come.

In Europe opposition to the status quo has traditionally tended to take the form of left-wing politics of some description. America, by comparison, never quite developed that revolutionary edge. There the confrontation is less between labour and capital, the bourgeois and working classes, than between the free and the uptight spirit. The country's (now institutionalized) rebels militate not so much against a 'ruling class' as against a style of life: the ideals of the earnest, hard-working, godly, sober-suited politician, businessman or functionary at whatever social level. The European rebel advocates some sort of alternative politics, usually a version of socialism. In America there is of course serious dissatisfaction with corporate behaviour, the shortcomings of welfare policy and the rest, but the biggest affront to their forefathers in the armory of the young is not their socializing agenda so much as their indolence, their hedonism, their refusal to take life seriously. Nothing could be more shocking to the American conscience than to benefit from the fruits of someone else's labour while deriding the work ethic that produced them.

The songs of British pop stars are replete with class politics, normally of a shallow kind, even when the singers are the privileged products of well-off backgrounds and private schools, as many are today. Their American counterparts, though left-inclined, tend to be more concerned with preaching the laid-back life than with class justice. Jack Kerouac's *On The Road* was not a highway to the socialist future, but a celebration of a Nirvana of relaxing drugs, guilt-free sex and endless booze. Social revolution can be a fraught, time-consuming business. Poking fun at Puritans is a lot more fun.

*

Like many a modern American the Puritans were great moralists. Which did not mean that their stances or behaviour were necessarily moral. The difference between moralism and morality is that morality is responsible: it takes account of human reality, it is not mere rhetorical goodness, and is not self-regarding. Moralism on the other hand is hypocritical by definition, since it disconnects the word from the act by making the practice of virtue impractical, by doing the opposite of what it preaches, by confining itself to making ineffectual, do-gooding noises, or by celebrating the moraliser's exquisite feelings.

Many an American politician has a preachy streak—Bush prominent amongst them—but the votaries of political correctness are the most obvious throwback to Puritan times. That is why PC attitudes originated where they did, and why they remain more virulent and pernicious in America than anywhere else. The virus of Puritan judgmentalism has traveled across four centuries, but is still astonishingly fit. Like the elect of New England the avatars of political correctness elevate themselves to the status of a caste of moral supermen, an elite of virtue, and cast into outer darkness anyone who is judged to stand outside their inexorable codes. What is distinctive about PC, American style, is the rigor of the creed, the self-monitoring it involves, the anxiety it induces, the climate of denunciation it breeds, the public shaming for offenders it brings, and the lack of proportion between the punishment and the crime. Most depressing of all is the cowering consensus such a climate can produce. Aggressive conformism, in the twenty-first as in the seventeenth century, and whether it takes place in the country club or the university faculty, continues to be an American characteristic.

No room is allowed for the weaknesses of human

nature or for the faintheartedness of the individual: 'Crook not God's rules to the experience of men (which is fallible and many times corrupt) but bring men unto the rule' as the Puritan preacher put it.[22] Public morality exists for the elevation of the citizen's soul, as well as the welfare of others, and sinning against it must be pursued and extirpated. In the case of PC the moral principles in question, such as equality for women or rights for homosexuals, may be no more objectionable in their intentions than New England laws designed to curb adultery or preserve public decency. What is reminiscent of the seventeenth century at its worst are the literal-mindedness of the accusers and the punitive spirit with which the principles are applied. Literalism is a habit of mind of a Bible-based culture, and on sex, race, and society the rules of correct thinking have the force of unwritten scripture. Like the Puritans at their most intolerant and intolerable, enforcers of correctness are 'precisionists': niggling, carping critics forever measuring the behavior of their fellows against the sacred texts, and finding it wanting. The wonder today is the extent to which this spirit persists in those who have long since ceased to read the bible, who have never read it at all, or who are militantly opposed to it.

So we reach a position where sloppy drafting in a newspaper article or a slip of the tongue in conversation betokens not mere carelessness, or lack of consideration for others, but a putrid heart. 'If thou hast no calling, tending to the public good, thou art an unclean beast.'[23] Such was the attitude of the Puritan sermonizer. If you fail to live up to our notion of the good society, says his PC reincarnation, you are a political reactionary and a moral moron. (There are obvious echoes between the title of Philip Roth's novel *The Human Stain,* whose hero falls foul of political correctness in academia, and the branding of the adulteress in Hawthorne's *The Scarlet Letter.*)

Fortunately correctness, American-style, can have a self-correcting mechanism, to the extent that it frequently evokes a virulent response. In ultra-tolerant Britain on the other hand PC seeps into the blood, drip by drip, like water into porous rock. The BBC is an example. After the massacres on the London Underground on 7 July 2005, in which 52 people died and 700 were injured, even when it was established that Muslim extremists were to blame an instruction went out that BBC correspondents were to refer to the perpetrators as 'the bombers.' On no account were they to speak of 'Islamic terrorists', since to do so might make moderate Muslims feel bad about themselves and their religion. In America a similar directive might well have been issued by the editor of this or that organ of the press. The difference is that, had it come to light, instead of being supinely accepted, it would have provoked a reaction, not least on the Christian Right. In this instance at least Puritanical extremes can have the inadvertent merit of balancing one another.

*

Intrinsic to political correctness is a fault-finding, lawyerly cast of mind. 'Lawyers, those devouring locusts'[24] was an early Puritan view of the profession, though in many respects New Englanders had only

PSYCHOSIS OF A NATION

themselves to blame. The mania for litigation was inherent in their culture. A prudential approach to life and a contentious spirit favoured a legalistic response to the smallest problems, and the church (like the law today) busied itself disproportionately with the minutiae of daily life. Close study of the scriptures were conducted in an argumentative spirit, sermonizing was an ideal school of advocacy, and the Manichaeism of Puritan doctrines encouraged the adversarial ethos typical of the Anglo-American legal systems.

The contract theory of human relations was already in existence, but the American Puritans gave it their special stamp. As a rule they were heavier on responsibilities than on rights, but the responsibilities cut both ways. The notion of the covenant, in effect a deal done with God whose terms and conditions were endlessly debated, embedded the legalistic approach to life deep in the Puritan spirit. The Covenant of Grace in particular was a lawyer's dream. Intended as a softening of the arbitrariness of predestination, it was a version of the Arminian heresy. The idea was that instead of simply submitting to God's inscrutable will, the individual could do a deal. The unwritten contract involved an undertaking to live a virtuous life and make the best of one's talents, in return for a promise of salvation. The lawyers/theologians involved commended themselves heartily on setting up the terms of the biggest deal anyone was likely to make. 'Never was there such a wise contrivance heard of in the world.'[25]

When it came to delivering the Good Lord himself was not without his obligations. After doing his level best to

live a saintly life the individual had the right to demand
that God come up with the goods. 'You may sue him of his
own bond written and sealed' said John Preston, one of the
authors of the covenant, 'And he can't deny it.'[26] The
Covenant of Grace helped make 'the deal' a metaphor for
the whole of human existence, and so, in American
parlance, it remains today.

America's tough approach to crime and punishment
was also there from the nation's infancy. (Not that the
England the settlers left behind was a model of
moderation. A social historian, Laurence Stone, has
described the period from 1500 to 1660, the end of the
Puritan era, as 'cold, suspicious, and violence-prone.'[27])
Intolerance of sin was in the Puritans' blood, and the
enormous US prison population is evidence of a
continuing urge for retribution. It is no accident that,
compared to European countries, America (and Britain)
are notably weak on rehabilitation. Forgiveness and
redemption in this world were never Puritan priorities;
chastisement was. To this day the assumption lingers that
criminals are outcasts from whom God has withdrawn his
mercy. It follows that there is little to be hoped from them,
and that the best solution is to isolate them from society
for as long as possible so as to minimize the harm they can
do to god-fearing citizens. Once they are seen as
predestined 'losers' it makes sense to concentrate on
keeping them out of circulation.

Any hopes of salvation rest not on training or
education to equip them to live more honest lives, but on
encouraging them to turn their hearts to the Bible. As
Governor of Texas it was George W. Bush who

introduced a faith-based prisoner reform programme, on lines pioneered by Charles Colson, of Watergate fame, who himself underwent a Christian conversion in the Seventies. The most interesting side of this programme was its intensive nature: Bible classes could take up the whole working day and last over a year. For those who stayed the course the rehabilitation rate, it was claimed, was impressive. What we do not know is the effect a full-scale programme of education and training might have had, as distinct from one aimed at the saving of souls.

America's reversion to capital punishment in recent years, at the very moment when it has been discontinued in Europe, would appear to illuminate a gulf in sensibility like nothing else. In seventeenth century Europe executions were of course common, frequently for petty crimes, but even then Anglo-American Puritan mores were distinctive. The most revealing aspect was their unattractive habit of hounding a condemned man with sermons to the gallows. Instead of being on hand to soothe his transition to the beyond, Puritan ministers would harangue the poor wretch literally to the grave. (In England a similar practice, which consisted of forcing the condemned man to listen to a sermon with a scull before him, persisted till the eighteenth century.)

Historically we tend to focus on the severity of Puritan justice, and on its most picturesque aberrations: the Salem witch trials of 1692, or the execution of two New Haven men accused of having sex with sows, whose guilt was confirmed by the court when both produced offspring that allegedly resembled their fathers. Yet as European defenders of the American legal tradition (and there are some) claim, it has more positive aspects. As well as a manifestation of its retributive spirit America's plague of lawyers can be seen as reflecting the Puritan predilection, evident in more humdrum early New England trials, for taking individual rights seriously, even within a harsh and sometimes superstitious regime. Nor would it be right to explain the severity of current practice—the death penalty, boot camps, 'zero tolerance', or the 'three strikes and you're out' approach to justice—simply in terms of Puritan repressive instincts. American delinquency levels are enormous, and high crime rates invite tough measures. So the first question must be: why is it that in a rich, god-fearing democracy that is the product of a Puritanical culture, crime should be some three times higher than in comparable countries?

Racial deprivation, poverty, ghetto life, inadequate education, organized crime by immigrants with a background in criminal cultures like the Mafia, are amongst the usual explanations, yet again the Protestant legacy has its role. Partly because of the equation between money, success and virtue, the flaunting of wealth is far more striking in America than in Catholic countries. (In France the done thing is to avoid *les signes extérieurs de richesse,* if only to fool the taxman.) The visual stimulus to acquire cash and goods exists everywhere, but nowhere more than in America, with its infinitely commercialized culture of temptation. High counts of delinquency have also been attributed to the peculiar pressures Americans are under to 'make it' at all costs.

According to this theory the very vibrancy of American

democracy, its cult of liberty and of the self-made man or woman, encourage a hell-bent scramble for wealth with no holds barred. (The obvious contrast is with Soviet and Chinese communism. With their lack of freedom, massive security apparatus, absence of financial structures and consumer goods and low expectations of the individual, there was relatively little personal crime. Even supposing you outwitted the authorities, if you can't use the spoils to buy a big house and car, flash your girls or take them for holidays in Barbados, what is the point?) Nor is it hard to see how the cult of individualism, carried to extremes, can conflict with social values and be perverted into crime. Seen this way the American society of opportunity the Puritans did so much to encourage is easily transformed into one where criminal enterprise, by a bank robber or a banker, can flourish.

*

'Two Negroes, four casks of brown sugar, two casks of cocoa and two pateraroes'[28] was how a Boston court once listed a person's worldly goods. By 1720 a sixth of the town's population's was black, though the New Englanders' devotion to the liberty of the individual does not appear to have influenced their attitudes to the race question overmuch. On this the Puritan conscience was less delicate than on other matters, and certainly less enlightened than that of their religious enemies, the Quakers. When it came to race the clash of principles with practice was there from the start. 'There shall never be any bond-slavery, villenage or captivity amongst us' the New

England law stated—with two exceptions: those who were caught in battle, and those who sold themselves to their masters.

This let-out clause enabled the Puritans to benefit from the forced labour of Indians caught in war, or still more dubiously sell them on to the West Indies, sometimes in exchange for black slaves. Given that their conduct towards the heathen Indians could be brutal—when they were not killing them and seizing their lands they were bribing them with rum—there was no lack of indentured labour doing service to the godly. (The fact that the New Englanders were the first to legislate against cruelty to animals underscores their inhumanity.)

Cotton Mather was in favour of the religious equality of blacks, and of providing them with education. Yet he thought it a mistake for them to seek freedom, believing that they were better off as they were. Like it or not (and there is little evidence that they worried about it too much) the Puritans were involved in a part-slave economy. New England makers of rum did not protest that the molasses they used was produced by slaves, and the cost of production in New England cotton mills was kept low by slave conditions in the South, which warded off higher-priced imports. In the eighteenth century the North did deals with the South which recognized slavery in return for commercial advantage.

The New England record was to an extent salvaged by the role played by the North in emancipation, when anti-slavery agitators like William Lloyd Garrison set up a newspaper, *The Liberator*, in Boston. The campaign often had strong religious overtones, directed as much at cleansing their souls from sin, one sometimes suspects, as to freeing them from slavery.

*

At times it seems that Puritan influence on contemporary American life can be easily assessed: that its virtues have been eroded to the point of obliteration, and all that is left are its unattractive aspects. At others one is more impressed by the sense of liberty, dynamism and mission that the Puritans played such a part in bequeathing to the nation. Most often it is hard to make up one's mind about the cost/benefit balance one way or the other, not least because of the contradictions inherent in the creed. The conflicts are such that you can only wonder how they can be reconciled in a single nation. And chief amongst them, perhaps, is sex.

3

SEXUAL NEUROSES THEN AND NOW

'I abhor the USA's prevailing sexual hypocrisy, and the shameful laxity it leads to.'

André Breton.

In America everything to do with gender takes on a manic aspect, and a glance back to the seventeenth century makes it easier to understand why. Nowhere are the paradoxes of the Puritan conscience more flagrant, more tragic and occasionally more entertaining than in the sexual sphere.

'My life is a rebellion against the Puritan stock early in my childhood, seeing the hypocrisy and the hurt in that, and the dreams being fed in motion pictures. Of course I've overcompensated for the repression.'

So spoke Hugh Hefner, founder of Playboy enterprises, in an interview a few years back in *The Times*.[1] A tenth generation descendant of a passenger on the Mayflower, his upbringing was Midwestern and his parents prohibitionists. On top of that he grew up during the Depression and World War Two. His claim that his free-wheeling way of life was an act of rebellion, and his quip about overcompensation confirm the obvious: that when sexual repression rules the reaction can take extravagant forms. As if to demonstrate the truth of this *The Times* shows him surrounded by seven young blondes at the age of 75.

Hefner's mention of the hurt and hypocrisy his Puritan upbringing caused suggests that we have more healthy attitudes today. A reasonable view, many will think, though looking at Playboy magazine some men and rather more women might wonder. Exploitation of women can cause hurt, we are frequently reminded, and the problem with America's Puritan legacy is that one kind of hypocrisy can easily replace another.

It might have come as a surprise to Hefner's septuplet of girls to learn that they owed their positions in his retinue, not to speak of the existence of Playboy itself, to the after-effects of sexual oppression in New England some four centuries ago. Another publication America owes to its Puritanical past is the Kinsey Report. Its objectivity has been questioned and its findings queried, but that is in the nature of the genre. The most interesting thing about it is not that women as well as men had a weakness for pleasuring themselves, that the average couple had sex two or three times a week in this or that position, or that there were homosexuals in 1940s America, something no sane person ever doubted. What is remarkable about the Kinsey Report is the fact of its existence. In no other country could a similar study have been produced, and nowhere else could it have caused the furore it did.

Like Hefner, Kinsey was the product of a Puritanical family, and like the *Playboy* owner his reaction to his upbringing took a dramatic, some might say over-compensatory form. Instead of breaking loose from the parental grip by taking a more relaxed view of sexual matters, as youngsters had been doing since Victorian times, he ricocheted, violently, to the opposite pole. In one thing he can be said to have followed in the family tradition: his father was a preacher and Kinsey Jr became a sermonizer himself—not just an advocate but a fanatic of sexual emancipation.

That much is understandable, but in his case things were more complex. The man who purported to provide America with scientifically compiled information on human sexuality was himself a sexually tormented soul. His claim was that he was helping America towards a saner approach, yet worries about his own identity (he was bisexual) lead him to mutilate himself in a peculiarly perverse way. Reading the details of his life only one conclusion is possible: that if you wanted a coolly objective assessment of America's sexual psyche the last people you would turn to would be the Kinsey family, *père* or *fils*.

Reactions to his study are as important as the report itself. The point is not whether Kinsey was saint or sinner, a hero who challenged the repressive codes of his day or a sexual neurotic in search of notoriety. It is better that people should know the facts about sex than not, even if some of Kinsey's facts appear to have been less than reliable, and his conclusions overblown. The real

questions are why such a report came about in the first
place, and why it evoked the hysteria that it did. Clearly it
was a blow against conservative America. How far it
succeeded in promoting more natural sexual mores is
another matter. It is not only Kinsey's personal history that
was strange; his voyeuristic behavior in the preparation of
his report, and his robotic approach to human intimacy,
were anything but normal. Equally unhealthy was the
mixture of prurience and indignation in the way the report
was received throughout the Anglo-American world.

To many the report came as a liberation, but freedom
has its disenchantments, in sex especially. Reading its ice-
cold tabulations of the frequency and variety of sexual
behavior, for the first time in their lives large numbers of
previously well-adjusted men and women must have
worried about how they were placed in the sexual
marathon. How would their record look in public? Were
they missing out? The average man and wife in small-
town America of the 1940s, till then persuaded that for all
their outward ordinariness their sex life was something
rather momentous, would suddenly have discovered that
they were unadventurous to a humiliating degree. Before
the report came out they might have been troubled by
occasional illicit desires; now they were more likely to
worry about their timidity, a concern that might or might
not be shared by their partner. As illustrated in the brief
Soviet experiment with free love in the 1920s, sexually
speaking people can only stand so much emancipation.

*

PSYCHOSIS OF A NATION

Hefner and Kinsey were at one in debunking what they rightly saw as cant and hypocrisy. Each in his way made a profession of it, and a lot of money. The evolution of sexual mores that the Kinsey Report accelerated created an atmosphere in which magazines like *Playboy* were not just big business, but business that could be presented as ethically based; for if there is one thing calculated to give us a warm glow of satisfaction it is the rejection of sexual conservatism. Amongst sophisticated folk the very mention of sexual Puritanism brings a wry, knowing smile. One reason for this is that Puritan inhibitions appear to us as comic, which indeed they sometimes were. Another is that it flatters the emancipated modern conscience to exaggerate the Puritans' fear of erotic pleasure. As it happens the facts about Puritans and sex are less damaging to their reputation than is generally understood.

From myths about Victorian England (Queen Victoria and Prince Albert shared a hearty sex life, not to speak of a taste for nude paintings, and piano legs were left scandalously uncovered) to the conviction that New Englanders were enjoined to practice sexual abstinence (they weren't, and their procreation was as prodigious as the Victorians'), sex lore about former times can be as gratifying as it is frequently dubious. To see the Puritans and Victorians as life-deniers and ourselves as life-affirmers is a cosy moral stance. If we were as relaxed about sex as we claim, why would we need to construct straw men out of the Puritans or Victorians, which we often do? Ribald overstatement is a factor, but then sexual humour can be a sign of self-consciousness—the very affliction we claim to have cured in ourselves. The fact that the Puritans had a rather more enlightened attitude to the erotic than we prefer to imagine comes as something of a disappointment, a blow to our self-esteem.

Talk of Puritanical sex conjures up thoughts of chastity, seclusion and self-denial, and there was something of all three in the Puritan persona. Yet that is to forget that a key element in the origins of Protestantism was a rejection of the monastic life. New England women may have been demurely dressed, but they were not secluded in nunneries, and the Puritans did not preach a nunnish renunciation of the world. These 'men of marble' were by no means unfeeling. Nor were they unworldly, and individual Puritan leaders could be as understanding as Catholics, if not as tolerant, when it came to the sins of the flesh. Lamenting sexual licentiousness Governor Bradford of Plymouth drew some shrewd and strikingly modern-minded conclusions.

'It may be in this case as it is with waters when their streames are stopped or damned up, when they get passage they flow with more violence, and make more noise and disturbance, then when they are suffered to rune quietly in their own chanels. So wickedness here being more stopped by strict laws, and the same more nerly looked unto, so as it cannot rune in a common road of liberty as it would, and is inclined, it searches every wher, and at last breaks out wher it getts vente.'[2]

The Governor's ruminations were not just wise, they were prophetic. The long-term effects of prudery and repression to which he alluded are still with us, and now that the sexual appetite has finally 'got passage' in Anglo-

American culture it flows more violently, and makes more noise and disturbance, than in historically more permissive countries, where it was allowed to 'rune quietly in its own chanels.'

Contrary to received opinion the Puritans were never opposed to sexual gratification; what they insisted on was that it stop short of uncontrolled passion and be lawfully received and given. They did more than tolerate sex: they taught that conjugal enjoyment was a God-given solace to humankind. Suspicious of sensuality, they were nonetheless in favour of marital erotic bliss. Difficult as it might be to believe, after a hard day's work on the farm Grant Wood's gaunt, righteous-looking couple would have had the sanction of the seventeenth century Church for comforting one another in bed. What made the Puritans nervous was not intercourse between married couples, even for non-procreative purposes: it was the thought of a natural, God-given instinct running out of control. The strength of their convictions about the innate human tendency to sin made them morbidly fearful of what they called 'libertine frenzies'.

The battery of laws they evolved to avoid this happening inevitably intruded into the intimacy of people's lives. Interfering as they could be, however, their prescriptions for a healthy sex life stopped short of those propagated by nineteenth century English clerics. These worthies cautioned against any but the missionary position, since any variation had more to do with lust than procreation, disapproved of women on top for reproductive as well as gender ranking reasons, and were strongly against entrance from behind, this being too reminiscent of man's animal nature. The Puritans never went that far, and often the interest they took in the marriage bed could be benign. 'Keep up your conjugal love in a constant heat and vigor', wrote Richard Baxter, a seventeenth century New England leader.[3]

Although their exhortations suggested that a woman's duty to attend to the needs of her spouse was greater than the other way round, they were not opposed to female sexual enjoyment. Speaking of 'The lawful delight allowed them by God'[4], Baxter made it clear that erotic pleasure was not confined to men. The same cleric was also realistic enough to recognize that men were more likely to impose on their wives in objectionable ways, thereby turning lawful delight into 'loathing and distain.' For the mid-seventeenth century, these were progressive notions in anyone's language. Even when combined with an element of moralizing, which it usually was, religious sanction of fleshly pleasure could be couched in crypto-erotic terms: 'God hath given us temporals to enjoy…We should therefore suck the sweet of them, and so slack our thirst with them, as to be not insatiably be craving after more.'[5]

As with alcoholic drink moderation was the message, and in the Puritan ideal of sex there was something both of the *honnête homme* and of the *homme moyen sensuel*. Like everything else a man's love-life had to be duly ordered. In their emotional world marriage was an organized, prudential affair (an attitude not totally unfamiliar to our own unromantic, 'pre-nup' times) and they were opposed to undue sexual passion, even between a man and his wife. What they wanted was love that burnt not too hot and with a steady flame, and no allowance was made for different sexual natures. It was a lot to ask of a human being, but it was done with the best of intentions.

Monitoring your erotic life in such a way as to gratify each other while not succumbing to physical or emotional excess requires an erotic thermostat that few possess. Yet the aim—of combining warmth and delight in the other with constancy towards them—was not such a crime against the species. A lot of what the Puritans believed about sex might be echoed by a marriage counselor forty or fifty years ago, though less of course today. Now they are more likely to suggest livening up a relationship by more frequent or less conventional sex, which is not what the Puritan preachers of delight in each other's bodies had in mind at all. For them the key to what we would call a happy sex life was self-control. This was part of their opposition to extreme moods of any kind: of fear turning to anger or warmth to passion. Passion is all-engrossing, and can possess those who feel it to the neglect of the feelings of those at whom it is directed.

Not that they were squeamish about public discussion of the facts of life. Many of these people lived rural lives, and on questions of public morality a certain earthiness could take over. Like today's Anglo-Saxon popular press, which combines indignant editorials on the decline of sexual morality with generously detailed examples of the degeneracy in question, their sermonizing could occasion-ally have a lubricious flavour. Before Kinsey masturbation was a taboo topic, but it was not thought too indecent to feature, in lightly veiled language, in seventeenth century pulpits or pamphlets. The subject recurred frequently in the diaries of young men. Cotton Mather himself admitted that 'Satan buffeted me with unclean temptations', to the point where he wanted to 'cut off my right hand.'[6] Instead he fasted, to little avail it seemed, and as an adult continued to rail against self-pollution.

Nor was there any pretence that the practice was confined to men. One such pamphlet—*Onania, or the Heinous Sin of Self-Pollution, and its Frightful Consequences in both sexes, Considered*—went through a suspiciously large number of editions. Fears about masturbation were one of the reasons the Puritans were opposed to making a fetish of virginity, which they saw as a 'popish trick.' What they feared was that if chastity were pushed to unnatural extremes, 'not being able to contain', youngsters would be driven to 'unnatural pollutions and other filthy practices in secret.'[7]

The ancient practice of bundling, in which courting couples were allowed to share the same bed fully clothed, was another tacit recognition of the realities of sexual life. 'Tarrying', as it was sometimes called, was their version of today's over-nighting. It took place mostly in far-flung rural places, and amounted to a chaste form of pre-marital sex. Though seen as an indecent practice, for a long time New England preachers passed over it in silence, and it continued into the late eighteenth century.

The fact that the Puritans sermonized about sex so relentlessly reflected their obsessively controlling natures. In another sense, however, it was natural: they were laying the ground rules for a theocratic society, rules that encompassed every aspect of life, and for all their emphasis on the importance of the individual conscience, as men of a moralizing disposition they were hardly likely to leave the carnal passions alone. And as Governor Bradford makes clear, in a sea-faring colony they had more than the usual problems of public order. Punishments notwithstanding, as court records show, settlers and sea-faring visitors devised all manner of ways to gratify their lusts.

There was a good deal of illicit sex, not least amongst servants who lived and slept cheek by jowl, or farm workers free to pursue their amorous trysts in the privacy of nature. Taverns that were half-way to brothels persisted despite Puritan efforts to root them out, along with problems about controlling children familiar to many a modern parent. Then as now the young were in the habit of 'absenting themselves out of the families whereto they belong in the night, and meeting with corrupt company without leave, to the great grief of their superiors.'[8] Given that the alternative recreation was 'sermon gadding', it is hardly surprising.

The persistence of sexual vice brought out the Puritans' pragmatic instincts. Adultery was punishable by death, but the penalties were rarely enforced; only three cases are recorded. More often offenders were whipped or fined, or like Hawthorne's adulterous heroine, labelled with the accusatory letter A. In general they favoured public shaming over harsher sanctions. If a baptism took place sooner than nine months after marriage the punishment was a public 'humbling', in which the Minister conducting the ceremony was to 'publickly note and declare out the fault to all the congregation.'[9] Such measures were severe enough in their psychological effects, and overall the

Puritans appear to have kept illicit behaviour in check, just as they appear to have done in England. In America there was no Elizabethan era against which to measure the key statistic in a society's sexual morality at the time—illegitimate births—but in the Cromwellian Commonwealth a much less severe regime than that of New England resulted in a striking fall.

But it was all a precarious balance. Lugubriously conscious of man's predisposition to sin, they did what they could to shield him from temptation. The notorious drabness of the New England dress code was not always voluntary. A statute passed in Massachusetts in 1634 warned that 'no person either man or woman shall hereafter make or buy any apparel, either woollen or silk, or linen with any lace on it, silver, gold or thread.' There was also a law banning more than one split in the overgarments of both men and women, the point being to avoid any undue display of the coloured cloth—perhaps even sinful silk—that might lie beneath. Sober dress was a barrier to vice, and regulation was needed to keep the devil at bay. The principle was not so outlandish—there are schools today that regulate the length (or rather brevity) of girls' skirts to an inch above the knee—though in the case of the Puritans it was adult dress they were controlling.

No lace, and only one slit, not two. Whether they were busying themselves with other people's sex lives, or devising means to prevent the clothes they wore from inciting fleshly desires, always there was this weighing and measuring, this perpetually calculating spirit. As the historian Edmund Leites comments, 'Their conduct had the meticulous and anxious character of obsessive behavior.'[10] It is often remarked that the most dismal side of Puritanism was its suppression of theatres, fairs and other traditional ways to enliven their often joyless lives. It is even more dismal to reflect that it was not so much the theatre itself that worried them, as the thought of men and women congregating together for purposes of pleasure. Behind their often sensible attitudes there was always, as H.L. Mencken wrote, the haunting fear that someone, somewhere may be happy.

*

Sexual repression and the subjugation of women usually go together. In New England this was not entirely the case, and prudery went along with a relatively enlightened attitude to women's rights. Feminism is frequently seen as a reaction against Puritan patriarchal values, yet in their more enlightened moments New Englanders could be pioneers in the field. The Puritans we look back on in self-righteous indignation, or with a wry smile, were in many ways ahead of the mother country, as well as Continentals, in their treatment of the second sex.

'Vain man is apt to think we were merely intended for the world's propagation, and to keep its human inhabitants sweet and clean, but, by their leaves, had we the same literature, he would find our brains as fruitful as our bodies...Most in this depraved age think a woman learned enough if she can distinguish her husband's bed from another.'[11]

So wrote Mrs Woolley, an Englishwoman, in a

pamphlet published in 1675. The Americans were more advanced than the England she pictured. A law was passed that not only prohibited husbands from beating their wives: they were forbidden to curse them. And that wasn't all. Heads of household were obliged to teach their dependents to read, not just wives but female children and servants, along with males. Clearly the intention was to encourage Bible reading, but there was a brisk trade in imported publications, and the result was that seventeenth century New England was probably the most literate society in the world. They also allowed women to inherit, a measure which—together with the relative scarcity of women amongst the early immigrants—made widows popular. Women took up responsible positions in society, often acting as merchants and traders in the absence of their husbands at sea.

The fact that the contract mentality was so developed was a factor in making marital law remarkably humane. The notion of the companionate marriage, which originated in England but was taken further in America, was another advance in the status of women. The patriarchal superiority of the male remained (at the time it was unthinkable that things should be otherwise) but rather than being a chattel, the woman became something closer to a partner. Sometimes this was literally the case: the Puritan couple were often in business together, running a family farm or shop. It has been suggested that we owe the very concept of home, with its regard for the covenant of marriage, its mutual duties and domestic sacraments, to the Puritan model. (A contemporary echo of this half-way house in progress towards equality is to be found in the ideas of the Council of Biblical Manhood and Womanhood,[12] who have developed what they see as a middle position between feminism and patriarchy. The idea is that, while men and women are equal, they are different because God has given them complementary roles in life, and this should be recognized in marital arrangements.)

When the covenant was broken, and divorce the only solution, Puritan thinking was realistic. Women were permitted to divorce a husband who was an adulterer, and were entitled to receive a third of their husband's estate.

'In case any married be convicted of such criminal uncleanliness as render them one flesh with another object than that unto which their marriage has united them, the injured party may sue and have their divorce from the offending...' A divorce being legally pursued and obtained, the innocent person that is released may proceed unto 'a second marriage in the Lord.'

Ironically, these enlightened attitudes to women were later to become a factor in the negative image of American femininity in Europe. The nineteenth century French were especially appalled. To them the typical American woman appeared an un-sensuous, domineering, uppity and altogether tiresome and fearsome creature. Not that the twentieth century American ideal of female beauty made any better impression: a French writer described Jayne Mansfield as 'the dream of some drunk Puritan at the tail end of an election banquet in the Mid-west.'[13]

*

So the Puritans were far from the patriarchal despots and sexual bigots we have frequently taken them to be. But repression breeds obsession in both the repressor and the repressed, and in rescuing them from caricature it would be wrong to depict them as comfortable with their erotic lives. 'Let thy lustful body be everlasting fuel for the unquenchable fire; let thy lascivious soul be eternal food for the never-dying worm' thundered one sermon.[14] Warnings like these were not designed to make men and women feel at home in their sexual skins.

Even when we have given them their due for their sexual realism, and their advanced thinking on women, overall the sexual legacy of Puritanism has been a disaster. Their ideals may not have been unreasonable but ideals were what they were. Individuals did what they could to live up to them and society did its best to enforce them, but the strain was huge, the prospects of success remote, and the negative effects lasting. Like class in communist countries sex in America was to become a national neurosis. And whereas in totalitarian regimes respite can sometimes be found in the personal and the private, the Puritan mindset was a kind of police state in itself, in which self-imposed vigilance continued in the most intimate moments. The individual was caught in a pincer between the community and his conscience, but conscience was the most unforgiving. Society's punishments could be harsh, but self-inflicted retribution, meted out for 'unclean thoughts' or some trivial peccadillo, could be harsher.

The proof of Puritan angst about sex was that they couldn't stop talking about it, and their preoccupations

showed in their vocabulary. The word 'carnal', indiscrim-
inately applied, was rarely off their lips. 'The carnal
multitude' was a favourite, referring to the base
materialism and animal appetites of the mass of men,
while 'carnal preaching' meant using an over-colourful
style in sermons—a sin because it meant appealing to the
congregation's low emotions. Incessant warnings bred a
chronic sense of guilt and internalized repression fed a
festering of desire. We have no means of knowing whether
they thought about sex as frequently as we apparently do;
there was far less erotic stimulus in those fustian times,
and far less leisure. Yet we know enough to suppose that
many a lonely, introverted soul must have lived on a
mental knife edge where sex was concerned, terrified that
his self-restraint could break down any moment, or that
the Lord might divine his fleshly thoughts. Sexual desire
was God-given—but how could they be certain what was
allowed and what wasn't? How was a man to know at
what point his urge to 'comfort' himself and his wife was
about to cross the unmarked frontier, and turn from God-
given solace to devilish lust? It was not only the
authorities who feared that the slightest relaxation would
lead to 'libertine frenzies.'

It is in their view of sex that the contradictory nature of
Puritan thought was most marked. Their attitude to
women was at once enlightened and confused. In a
straightforward patriarchal system the lines of authority
were clear: 'He for God only, she for God in him' the
English Puritan Milton had written. In New England this
was an unsustainable creed. Once his wife was educated,
and became a partner rather than a chattel, with a right to

divorce and to her own sexual feelings, how was a husband to maintain his patriarchal status?

Discipline was seen as the answer to every dilemma, and their mania for self-control gave them a horror of unstable temperaments. The irony is that anxious self-monitoring was not conducive to the calmness of spirit they preached, and their suffocation of human instincts could lead to the emotional instability they feared. Their case for marriage based on prudence rather than passion made a kind of sense, though it could lead to the dissociation of sex from feeling; something that, for different reasons, we lament today.

The Catholic view was that man was expected to sin because he was frail, but that his guilt could be erased through repentance, forgiveness and release. The Puritans demanded more of themselves, and of each other. Instead of absolution there was absoluteness: any lapses or excesses were sins for which no understanding could be expected. Their belief in the perfectibility of man's behavior made them more idealistic than the Catholics, yet they laid more stress than Catholicism on the irredeemably sinful human condition. Another contradiction. The way to bridge the gap was by a level of self-discipline granted to few mortals. They were being asked to do a near-impossible thing: repress their desires and emotions not only in public but in the most intimate moments of their lives. The consequences, in retrospect, are clear enough. A conscience chafing against the bars of its sexual prison produced an inflamed libido. The Puritans' insistence on chaste thinking and behaviour easily led to its opposite: prurience and excitability in everything touching sex or the erotic. Which is where we are today.

Puritan society was destined to buckle under its self-imposed constraints. By the mid-eighteenth century the impetus to liberty had asserted itself and a greater worldliness had taken over. But the New England experience was formative and its repercussions on the American sexual psyche remain powerful. Sexual liberation, fashioned in opposition to the Puritan cast of mind, bears the imprint of its origins. The same is true, to a lesser degree, in Britain, and the Anglo-Americans have the Puritans to thank for their neuroses, not least perhaps the taste for sado-masochism. Echoes of New England are equally discernible in the more extreme doctrines of feminism, where the vehemence that can characterize the movement recalls the preachiness, obsessiveness and intolerance of the early Puritans.

A look back over recent centuries suggests that the cyclical nature of sexual customs is well established. In early seventeenth century Puritan England pre-marital chastity increased. In England and America the eighteenth century saw a relaxation of standards, accompanied by an increase in sex before marriage and a consequent surge in the number of illegitimate children. In the late eighteenth and nineteenth centuries came a new wave of moralism, followed by twentieth century permissiveness, and in America today another attempt to turn back the clock is once again in progress. It is in the nature of Puritanism, with its innate tendency to excess and its inner contradictions, to produce violent swings, as one absolute gives rise to another. Once the reins are relaxed, an over-harsh morality can be followed by a cynical immorality, in which the feelings of women in particular count for nothing. A sudden release from constraint can lead to an ethical vacuum, of the kind we are currently witnessing in former totalitarian countries like Russia, and to a lesser extent China. Puritanism, at its most paranoid and controlling, could have totalitarian aspects, and the collapse of its ethical system can lead to a similar void.

Puritanism in sex is a mental ailment for which an antidote has yet to be invented. If a single word were needed to characterize the sexual atmosphere of New England, as well as of contemporary America, it would be overwrought. It is in the reaction to Puritanism that our sexual enlightenment lies, but also our pathologies. Purist approaches to sex, censorious or libertarian, share a similar cast of mind, and once enclosed in its thinking you never quite escape the circle.

*

In today's America the seventeenth century sexual conscience has been blown apart by the contradictions it secreted. Now absolute freedoms are demanded in the same self-righteous spirit as the Puritans insisted on absolute repression, and the result is that sexual libertarianism is becoming as unsustainable as prohibition. Determination in Anglo-Protestant cultures to dispense with the inhibitions of the past has begun to assume the earnestness and intolerance characteristic of the progenitors of their problems. 'Self-realization' can be a pretext for promiscuity, and 'discarding inhibitions' another name for sexual egotism, exhibitionism or self-indulgence. Obviously the commercialization of sex has always been there, even in New England, where it took the form of prostitution or indecent books or prints, but it would be absurd to claim that there is any real parallel with a blatant and ubiquitous business that is becoming a major social problem, not least for feminists.

It has taken a long time for the Anglo-Americans to loosen up on the sexual front to the extent they have, and now that it has happened there is no stopping them. France, a sexual Mecca for Britons and Americans in the eighteenth and nineteenth century, is staid by comparison. (Another field where the British and Americans have discovered their freedoms belatedly, and become mightily excited about it, is contemporary art. Forms of expression conceived in Paris or Moscow almost a century ago are today promoted as daringly original, Anglo-American inventions, to be greeted with indiscriminate acclamation by an over-heated market. Gore Vidal has remarked about art that everything changes except the avant garde. The same, he might have added, is true of sexual innovation.)

Like Hugh Hefner with his seven blonds, or Kinsey with his sexual crusading, contemporary America is in over-compensatory mode. The instability Puritan thinking engendered has reached chronic proportions, as the America finds it impossible to strike a balance. In anything touching on human sexuality a giddy sequence of reactions and counter-reactions are America's steady state, and in recent decades the swings of opinion have accelerated to the point where libertarian and conservative crusades overlap. The result is a chaos of contradictions. Amongst other things this explains why the Anglo-

Americans have developed a culture of sexuality that has reached unprecedented levels of licence while continuing to pillory their leaders for the slightest irregularity in their private lives. At that point they revert to Puritanical standards. Individual citizens assert with growing insistence their own and other people's right to do as they please in the privacy of their homes, but when it comes to the dalliances of public figures the media 'publickly note and declare out the fault to all the congregation.'

Confusion about standards is clear from the rules and conventions governing the sexual content of films and television. A distinction between what can be said and what can be seen operates in most cultures, but here again America goes to extremes. Verbally (i.e. sex in the head) it is possible to get away with virtually anything, as *Sex and the City* shows, but the series that features four women chatting about anal sex or the taste of sperm would find itself in trouble if a single female nipple were by chance to be exposed. On French or Italian public television the talk is less raunchy, though the viewer is more likely to be confronted with the nipple. Protestant thinking on sex has produced a situation where the most blatant discussions of erotica are increasingly seen as normal, while the sight of a woman's breast is a carnal affront to our most civilized sensibilities. The same perverse values, confusing the natural and unnatural, explain why taking a bath with their children or photographing them naked can inspire the fear of God in many an American father.

*

It took a French aristocrat—de Tocqueville—to give us the most revealing account of American democracy, and one of the most perceptive exposés of Protestant sexual deformations in recent times has come from the pen of an Italian-American woman. Camille Paglia has a tough and telling line of criticism, not just for conservatives but the new Puritans of the feminist left, whom she sees as their allies. Detecting a Puritan antisepsis in the way liberals in general have taken to discussing sex, she used a report by The Special Committee on Human Sexuality of the Presbyterian Church to make her case.

Keeping Body and Soul Together called for a major change in Christian attitudes, and approved of homosexuality and extra-martial relationships. 'The old Protestant ethic, masquerading in new hip clothes' is Paglia's verdict. She sees the report as a banal, simplistic, naïve, anti-erotic and generally reactionary document. 'Its unctuous normalizing of dissident sex is imperialistic and oppressive', writes Paglia, its dominant tone one of 'aggressive compassion'[15].

As always it is a pleasure to watch Paglia go to work, and this time it is easy to see what steamed her up. The report is indeed provoking, in a way the clerics who wrote it were clearly unable to anticipate. Keen to be seen as radical, they succeed only in being patronizing: liberal pietists who hand out sexual licence like tablets to be taken twice a week. No one can kill off joy in sex more quickly than the church, and the report's *de haut en bas* permissiveness is chronically de-tumescent. Reading it gives a taste of what it must have felt like for New England husbands to be informed from the pulpit that it was the will of God that they should sleep with their wives; after that they may no longer have felt the desire. The report even includes those little touches of lubricity old-time preachers would throw in to keep the congregation awake. Harold, confined to a hospital respirator, wants his wife 'to express their sexual intimacy' by performing oral sex on him, and is assisted by the chaplain, who secures their privacy.

Paglia hits her targets with brio, though not even she is immune to the workings of the Puritan retrovirus. For her it is not enough to insist on the naturalness of the erotic. Sex must be the diametrical opposite to everything New England believed—untamed, orgiastic and pornographic—and the backsliders and timid of spirit must be harangued till they see the light:

'Pardon me: I happen to think that Italian opera and African-American rhythm and blues contain the real truth about sex, with its Dionysian energies and ungovernable intensities.'[16]

Suddenly we are back to the finger-jabbing, evangelical style as Paglia, Latinate priestess of sex, insists that Italians and African-Americans know things that no one else does. These are the sexually elect, chosen people to whom the truth about human eroticism has been vouchsafed, and it behoves us to listen. In her writings and public addresses her aggressive eroticism hammers away at the *homme moyen sensuel* in the congregation, reducing the men to a state of angst because they have never felt tempted to try on their mothers' dresses, and the women to feelings of inadequacy because their only lovers have been white American males, not all of them overwhelmed by ungovernable intensities in their sexual lives, and some of them only moderately enthused by opera.

If America Paglia's celebration of passion was thought shocking. In Paris, Rome or Madrid it would have provoked embarrassment, not because of it's audacity but because, like a matriarch's warblings about the splendours of love, it is one of those things that just doesn't need to be said. Even in Britain her hymns to the flesh would have an antiquated ring. Already in the 1920s D.H. Lawrence was going on about phallic consciousness, and Paglia's sexual proselytizing comes across like Lawrence recorded to a synthesized beat. Though Lawrence, at least, was being true to himself and his times. Work that was once deemed pornographic (such as *Lady Chatterley's Lover*) sprang from a search for sexual liberty of expression in the face of a genuinely repressive ethos. America's post-Puritan thrill-seeking, on the other hand, can owe as much to the urge for exhibitionism and phony 'transgression' as to true desire.

As with her overheated enthusiasm for Madonna (whom Paglia praises for her 'animality') and for Robert Mapplethorpe, one wonders how much of Paglia's rapture is a stagy defiance of prudes and how much is truly felt? It is sad to see people from non-Protestant backgrounds, with the potential for promoting more mature attitudes to sex, end up imprisoned in the Puritan dialectic, a system of thought condemned to be forever reacting against itself. Her evangelical spirit has not tempered with age. Now 58, in a recent interview her pulpit style descended into incoherence of a revealing kind.[17] On the one hand she insisted that the 1972 documentary Deep Throat was 'an epochal moment in the history of modern sexuality.' (Deep Throat was a porno movie about a woman who discovers that she has a clitoris in her throat.) Next she lamented the loss of feminine mystique in films:

'The only thing that's going to bring sex back to movies is if people start dressing in a more covered-up manner because that's the whole point—recreate taboo.'

No better illustration of the Protestant cycle of sex could be imagined. In the space of a decade or so Paglia has done the whole circle: from a reaction against Puritanism in its conservative and liberal manifestations to an exaltation of pornography and primeval lust, then to the recreation of taboo by means of covering-up. And once the taboo is back in place we can begin the circle again.

*

The Puritan heritage and the counter-currents it provokes have produced a sexual civilization permanently out of sinc, as the American psyche is trapped in an endless oscillation between guilt and exuberance. (The nineteenth century French writer Barbey d'Aurevilly, a fierce critic of Puritanism, wrote presciently of its tendency to 'erupt in caprice.'[18]) It is not a question of the centre not holding; in America there never was a centre. The furore over gay rights is emblematic in this respect. Despite a new and somewhat self-conscious openness, seen in the round attitudes towards homosexuality are as moralistic as ever they were. The difference is that instead of condemnation the talk is now of 'celebration', as homosexuality has gone in the space of a few decades from being a very bad thing to a very good thing. In a Protestant culture what it cannot be is a thing. Always there has to be disapproval or applause.

The casualness about sex that conservatives deplore and liberals celebrate is suspect for similar reasons. Whatever the fundamentalists fear and Camille Paglia exalts America is not about to become a pagan nation. Paganism suggests insouciance, the last word to describe attitudes in a country where religion has ensured that sexual self-consciousness remains rooted in the national being. An absence of naturalness about sex is not corrected by a no less nervy libertarianism, or the commercialization of desire. The distance from Puritan repression to exhibitionist freakery is short. One may be a form of release from the other, but both are pathological behaviour.

Determined to throw off its legacy of guilt and introspection, America affects a nonchalance about sex it does not feel. This helps to explain the new religion of the 'cool.' Borrowed from black culture, it is a term with many overtones, including at its best self-respect, a right to difference, and a refusal to be flustered or defensive. Its recent usage is connected with jazz (*Birth of the Cool*, Miles Davis's landmark recording in the late Forties, symbolized the mood: laid-back, unhurried, playing behind the beat), and with indolence-inducing narcotics. In the past the word had ambiguous connotations in the English tongue (the Regency fop Beau Brummell was described as 'cool and impertinent') but now it has become wholly approving. Everyone and everything in America now claims to be easy, relaxed, playing behind the beat—and much of it is phony. The one thing no Puritan has ever been is cool. 'A man at ease with himself' warned a seventeenth century divine, 'is a man lost'.[19]

'No problem' says the modern white American, endlessly, 'I'm cool with that.' The insistence of this *désinvolture* has something of the force of a denial. If he or she is so open-minded about everything, so terminally relaxed, why stress it so much? For the average white American Protestant usually there *is* a problem, perhaps of a sexual nature, and nine times out of ten the last thing he or she feels about it is cool. Their mimicry of African American parlance suggests a desire to escape their own origins. Which gives the whole game away. If white America did not have a problem with itself and its traditions it would not ape the externals of another culture as a form of instant liberation.

Amongst young (and not so young) Americans the black vernacular about coolness in all its connotations has become a quasi-universal argot. On pre-marital sex, one parent families, abortion, homosexuality and the rest, clearly their views are genuinely more open and relaxed than those of their grandparents. But affectation plays its part, and whatever their deeper feelings a stance of ironic detachment and an attitude of irreverence are compulsory. (In America few people will trust you unless you are irreverent, Norman Mailer has remarked.) A flamboyantly free-wheeling attitude to sex has become de rigueur. But in Protestant cultures mindsets change more on the surface than beneath, and for all their heavily accentuated libertarianism new types of conformism can emerge to replace the old.

In Americans were truly relaxed about sex they would not go on about it, like the Puritans before them, as much as they do. Even when attitudes and actions are liberated the sex that results can be curiously un-sensuous, and redolent of Puritan utilitarianism. With its prudential aspects (mutual tests for AIDS, prenuptual agreements) and matter-of-fact discussion of mechanics America's approach to sexual matters can be the opposite of what it claims. Far from being laid-back it appears endlessly garrulous, puritanically hygienic and—as the alarmingly slimmed down TV character Ally McBeal exemplifies— more neurotic than erotic.

Friends is another example of a TV programme that, while apparently free and easy, manages to be devoid of sensuality. The very title has sanctimonious overtones ('just good friends'). 'Relationships' are a permanent subject of conversation, but in a nervy, jokey way, as if the entire cast were teenage virgins. In good Puritanical style there is never the least hint of lust or passion, and when it is suggested that one character has had sex with another, you don't believe it. Abstinence is the key to their behaviour. No one smokes or is tempted to smoke. No one drinks or is drunk. No one is fat or even a little podgy. No one takes drugs, and the idea of one of them contracting a sexual disease is unthinkable; the worst health risk they are exposed to is an overdose of cafein. And for all their various adventures their temperaments remain unflagging- ly equitable: the characters are to a large extent inter- changeable and all are basically nice. These are mechanized folk, perfected people, as godly as human life gets, Puritanical figures in contemporary guise. At the end of this line of human development lies the cyborg Lara Croft, the ultimate sexual expression of the Protestant conscience: abstract, un-carnal, emotionally neutral, a hygienic surrogate for the genuine, messy, un-Puritanical thing.

Sex and the City reflects a different kind of Puritanical thinking. A reaction against namby-pamby stuff like *Friends,* it is another example of Puritanism inverted: self-consciously raunchy and extravagantly contrived. We are supposed to view it as the lives of four young New York women with the veneer of respectability stripped away. Yet even after allowance is made for humorous exaggeration, as critics have noted the sexual activity is promiscuous in a way that few young women's lives actually are. More plausible is the nature of their relationships, which are highly calculated, to the point where the entire show can be read as a satire on the sexual economy. The characters emerge as autonomous agents bartering themselves and their attractions as commodities. Puritan discipline has given way to extreme freedom, but erotic libertarianism retains a prudential edge. What comes across are not the emotional ties between male and female but their ultimate isolation. All is disguised beneath a brittle patina of humour, but there is hardness beneath.

Such programmes are about winners in life's sexual race. Glamorous, smart, with good figures, the characters are never lost for partners. The opposite are the guests on the Jerry Springer show. Morally destitute, with no social graces, they lead what the Puritans called a random existence. Lacking all forms of self-control, their lives are given over to ruinous self-indulgence: fast-food, drinking, smoking, physical abuse and indiscriminate sex. Worst of all in modern eyes, they have lost control of their figures. These are the fat 'losers', as opposed to the skinny 'winners' of *Friends*. They are society's damned, put on public display like freaks in a medieval fair, for our entertainment and edification. Like the fornicators of New England who were made to stand under the gallows, their purpose is to remind us, by mockery, of the wages of sin.

*

By its stress on the individual, Puritan discipline turned into its opposite—freedom. This was progress. Now that America is a mass society governed by mass media, a less welcome change has taken place, as moral and commercial pressures turn individual freedom into liberty to conform. Choice and diversity are watchwords, yet everything from clothes to musical and sexual tastes is strictly codified and rigorously monitored. In Britain class convention remains all-powerful, and the more anti-elitist the conventions the more regimented they tend to be. America's classes are less clearly defined, though the powers of advertising and an ethos of conformism can produce similar, homogenizing effects.

To discuss such things in terms of cultural conflict is to miss the point. It matters little whether the codes of dress or behaviour are of the conservative or counter-cultural kind. Whether the baseball cap is worn frontwards or backwards, or no cap is worn at all, is immaterial; the one thing that is not allowed is to dress as you like, and few do. Departures from the norm are instantly noted and (amongst the young especially) ridiculed and punished by shaming devices less ferocious than those of New England, but in effect not so different. In this supposedly free and easy sub-culture tolerance is minimal. American popular culture has become a democratic theocracy and the Lord help anyone who goes against prevailing styles. Once it is decided who or what is on top, liking (or disliking) this film star/these trainers/those pants/that pop song is not permitted. Advertising is fashion's enforcer, and those most full of their independence are the ones most likely to dance to the stylistic imperatives like puppets on a string. Hag-ridden by legacies of conformism and in thrall to commercialized values, counter-cultural or otherwise, the average American is far from the free agent he or she would claim to be.

The tyranny of styles and manipulation by manufacturers are especially evident in pop. Whatever its musical value, with its adversarial ethos and strong erotic charge much of it expresses joy and release. But the hedonism and liberty the music celebrates express themselves in inflexible codes of language and conduct that militate against the individualism it preaches. That is why a roomful of people clubbing looks and sounds virtually identical the world over. The cliché is that unlike previous generations today's parents are 'letting the kids be themselves'. Yet that is exactly what does not happen. 'Letting them be like everyone else' would be a more honest sentiment.

The marketability of youth, and the fact that those in middle age are themselves the product of the Sixties, means that these values are no longer confined to the young but spread across generations. In Puritan times young children were dressed much like their parents, so as to give them, prematurely, the accoutrements of age and respectability. As grown-ups affect the clothes, the music and the literature of their children, now it is the other way round. In neither era are people encouraged to be themselves, to act their age, or to be different. Instead they conform to what is expected of them. Original spirits and genuine non-conformists do of course exist. Generally however the impression is of a kind of antinomian consensus that operates across generations. The Puritans in their time were rebels who became conservatives. 'Rebellion' today has become a civic duty.

*

A Puritan cleric visiting San Francisco or Los Angeles would have an eye-opening experience. To him it would seem that his worst fears had been realized: the nation was evidently in the grip of 'libertine frenzies' and of a wholesale surrender to the carnal life. Though not everything was lost. Listening to evangelical conservatives on the car radio as he made his way from Sodom to Gomorrah would encourage him in his hopes for a Great Sexual Awakening in which the moral order would be re-established. What he could never be brought to understand is that, largely because of the mindset bequeathed to America by people like himself, a religious crusade against sexual turpitude would most likely have the reverse effect.

The kind of 'back to basics' campaign the evangelicals

appear to want would not produce a society cleansed of sexual sin. It is the basics—i.e. America's religious inheritance in sexuality—that are the problem. It follows that going back to them would make things worse. America reacted against Puritan censoriousness and inhibitions by becoming a manically sexualized society. Far from exorcising her demons, a reversion to the Protestant sexual ethic would recreate the old tension in modern form. The most predictable result would be a backlash against the backlash, and a competition in self-righteousness between libertarians and fundamentalists, some of which we are already seeing, has few attractions. A re-run of Sixties self-indulgence dressed up as a defence of sexual rights would be a particularly tiresome prospect, and we are beginning to see that too.

No one, the new generation of feminists included, doubts that extreme sexual licence can have damaging effects on individuals and society, but the idea that a full-scale counter-reformation is called for is dubious for the simplest of reasons. A society cannot un-know what it knows. Reversing sexual liberation would be like dis-inventing nuclear weapons. The word is out about sexual deviancy and the rest, and it cannot be forgotten. It is not so many years ago that a large number of people were not aware that Lesbianism, transsexuals and sadomasochism existed, and so far as they may have suspected they did, their awareness was buried in a sub-conscious abhorrence. But they do exist, and have always existed, along with a host of more recondite sexual practices. Knowledge about them, along with technical information about more everyday sexual matters, has become an acquired right.

A key objection to the Christian Right are its obscurantist instincts. On gay rights we are referred back to the biblical texts, but homosexuality is a prime example of where the Bible has little to offer in the way of rational guidance for the twenty first century. Bible literalism means that we take its teachings at its word, yet all that it tells us about homosexuality is that the gospels are badly out of date. 'Tis the last advice we have had from heaven for now sixteen hundred years', the Puritan leader Cotton Mather ruefully reflected in another context,[20] and biblical strictures against homosexuality are passé in a literal—i.e. scientific—sense. Texts are disputed to and fro, but the only question that matters is what the Bible would have said about homosexuality had its compilers been aware that it is largely genetic.

For the New Englanders it was an abhorrent practice, and the few cases recorded were dealt with severely. Had they known about homosexuality what they knew about inoculation against smallpox, or Newton on gravity—issues they had little difficulty in reconciling with their faith—the Puritans, admirably open-minded when it came to scientific progress, might have had pause for thought. Seen historically the debates on abortion, or on stem cell research, throw up similar paradoxes. Religious fundamentalists who oppose abortion are perceived as hopelessly retrograde, Puritanical figures. But their seventeenth century forbears would not necessarily have been averse to abortion, if only as a measure of social control. The harsher side of their nature would probably have led them to see it as a possible solution to the problem of the poor having an uneconomic number of

117

children. One thing we can be sure of is that, like pre-war Sweden and Hitler and early socialists like H.G. Wells, they would have been attracted by eugenics.

On sex the different aspects of the Puritan tradition are continuously at war with themselves. This makes debates on homosexuality to a large extent artificial. Those who get fired up on the question would have us believe that the choice is between gay marriage on one hand and out-and-out condemnation on the other. As in heterosexual questions, however, the problem is not one of whether to tolerate or outlaw this or that practice (always excepting paedophilia, bestiality and so on); it is about how to accommodate minority sexual activities within the civil law. God's judgment on the matter we may or may not encounter later.

Solutions that infringe neither the institution of marriage nor the natural rights of homosexuals are perfectly possible to achieve. Within that range it is normal for secularists and for the adherents of this or that religious movement to hold differing views. What is illegitimate are attempts by Christians to impose on society fundamentalist attitudes that would criminalize a sexual orientation which by their own terms is God-given. For believers, as for atheists, sexuality has its spiritual aspect. Churches have a legitimate role in the debate, providing their responses to homosexuality and other aspects of human nature deal with the world as it is—an approach the Puritans themselves pursued at their most enlightened.

Sexual liberation cannot be put back in its box. The human personality has expanded, not always sinfully, and the box no longer fits. Even where more controls may be necessary an evangelical strategy would be likely to prove counter-productive. Pornography is the best example. Its prevalence in America owes much to factors that, if not unique, are characteristic of America's Puritanical culture, which has resulted in a prurient approach to sex. Personal freedoms guaranteed by the first amendment—themselves in part a legacy of New England individualism—are another. An enterprising and lightly regulated market economy which has helped to generate a huge sexual industry is a third. In the commerce of sex Puritan capitalism, Puritan freedoms and Puritan neuroses are neatly brought together. An evangelical approach would change none of these factors. And unless they are changed neither the demand nor the supply of pornography would be likely to diminish.

In the unlikely event of conservative evangelicals prevailing, and the introduction of drastic legislation, America could look forward to a rise in the social sicknesses associated with Prohibition, and more recently drugs: corruption, blackmail, gangsterism, murderous turf wars and the rest. And in the case of pornography, unlike what happened under Prohibition, there seems little prospect of driving down consumption. As Governor Bradford observed, 'So wickedness here being more stopped by strict laws, and the same more nerly looked unto, so as it cannot rune in a common road of liberty as it would, and is inclined, it searches every wher, and at last breaks out wher it getts vente.' Repressive legislation would also fail the pragmatic test. In contemporary America, where communication technology is so sophisticated and so widely available, pornographic imagery would have little trouble in 'getting vent.' If the communist regime in China has difficulty controlling the Internet it seems unlikely that a democratic American government could do better.

Clearly everything must continue to be done to limit access to pornography by children, and to discourage Hollywood and television companies from a cynical resort to sex and violence. But these are things that must be worked at patiently, persistently, pragmatically, over time.

*

A return to the model family is another priority of the Christian Right. In a society where some fifty percent of marriages end in breakdown or divorce, and where the children of the least well-off, often in black communities, suffer disproportionately, moves in this direction are surely desirable. The question is, what is practicable? The era of the Puritan patriarch cannot be brought back: the idea of a wife having towards her husband a 'noble and generous fear, which proceeds from love'[21] has had its day. Again a civil rather than a religious approach is most likely to succeed. If external signs of piety—churchgoing, church weddings, claims of the centrality of religion to daily life and so on—were a determinant of behavior then the more pious the state the lower its divorce rate would be. A glance around the country shows that the opposite is the case. Liberal Massachusetts has a divorce rate of 2.4, conservative Texas 4.1. The pattern between the Bible Belt and the less conservative states holds generally good: the greater the godliness, it would seem, the more divorces.

Gestures encouraged by some evangelicals, such as the renewal of the marriage vows in the form of a covenant, would be just that: gestures. The term 'covenant' recalls the Puritan belief that God had personally fashioned the institution of marriage, and that husband and wife must stick to the rules. 'No fault' divorce makes it easier to get round them, but then that was the intention. The idea of strengthening marriage by a covenant is little more than a declaratory device. Even in religious terms it has little meaning. The idea is to re-involve God in the partnership, yet if that is the aim the terms of the covenant are oddly un-ambitious. By restricting the grounds for divorce to adultery, sexual abuse and imprisonment, it appears to echo the declaration on marriage by the seventeenth century Cambridge Ministers.[22] Yet this gives a false impression of severity. Unlike the original the modern covenant is not legally binding; its only commitment is to seek counselling before marriage and before any divorce.

The whole idea turns out to be theologically as well as practically suspect. By passing itself off as a covenant in the solemn religious tradition it offends against Christianity and common sense. It seems fitting that Bible Belt Arkansas, whose Governor Mike Huckabee has been the most high-profile individual to take the covenant to date, has the third highest divorce rate in the country.

*

'There cannot be any progress (true progress, that is to say moral) except within the individual and by the individual

121

himself' Baudelaire wrote.[23] The French poet—no model of morality in his own life—was right and wrong. An improvement of public morality through the efforts of authority is possible. It happens in totalitarian systems. It happened in England during the Puritan reign, where the illegitimacy rate fell from 4% amongst the rural population during the Elizabethan period to half a percent at the height of Puritan influence—an extraordinarily low figure by any standards. The question is: how did they do it? Some of it was achieved by exhortation to the lower classes from above, and by a call to conscience, but religious admonition was backed by social control. One means of enforcement was for the midwife to interrogate the offender during labour, refusing to help the suffering woman give birth until she had divulged the father's name. An effective method, no doubt, and a handy means of ensuring that the father contributed to the child's upkeep, but not one that is available today.

The social context has changed utterly and irretrievably since the times when the church dictated public morals. Enforcement of the kind the American Puritans used, such as public shaming for adultery, would be both inhumane and inefficient: like it or not people are less easily shocked than they were. Nor are they as deferential: those lower down the scale no longer take the lead in their moral lives from their betters, and the young enjoy greater freedom than at any point in history, untrammelled by the first generation of parents to have made the break in the Sixties. Above all there is the freedom conferred on women by the use of the pill—another scientific discovery that is not going to be dis-invented.

Then there is the impact of prosperity on the moral manners of the times. The Puritans were afraid that too much money and too little to do would undermine the moral conscience, and they were right. That is how human nature works. Unprecedented levels of wealth, leisure and liberty are unlikely to prove conducive to chastity and self-restraint. This was never the case with aristocracies in the past. The correlation between luxury and debauchery in the leisured classes was at least as high as it is today, and the newly affluent middle or working classes are unlikely to behave any better. Add to that media and commercial pressures, and an increase in sexual recreation in all its forms becomes a bonus—if that is the word—of a successful, neo-liberal economy. Which itself is an indirect result of Puritanism.

So the circle turns. Godliness is demonstrated by industry, but industry engenders materialism. As wealth expands, so do the opportunities and temptations to use it for sexual comfort or adventure. In theory such temptations should be repressed, but the sweetness of the object desired grows with the repression, and when the strain becomes intolerable and the lure of the forbidden grows, constraints snap and repression ricochets into licence. In Puritan times the well-to-do were enjoined not to misuse their wealth by patronizing 'stewes, whore houses and brothell houses', or to indulge in 'Excess, gaudiness and fantasticalness' in their living arrangements. It was fine to make the money, but sinful to show 'inordinate affection unto the world'[24] .

In other words the New England rich were permitted to accumulate capital, but not to enjoy the fruits. Short of becoming a public benefactor and private saint (there were and are such people, but hardly a majority) what was a man of money to do? What was demanded of him was the modern equivalent of asking a successful businessman to re-invest all his profits, except for that portion destined for charity, build no mansions, indulge in no gourmet food or wines and certainly avoid multiple marriages, lap-dancing bars, expensive women or anything of that nature. In other words it was demanding the impossible. Where capitalism and sex were concerned the Puritans were destined to be hoisted high on their own petard.

*

Nowhere outside America is there more concern for equality of the sexes, and nowhere is there more angst and edginess in relations between men and women. In Protestant America sensuality, hovering between restraint and release, is forever tormented. The Puritans saw man as half human and half animal, and for them an excess of sexual feeling was a bestial disease. Today sexual liberation is seen as a psychic cure-all. America's Puritanical past has set the pendulum of guilt and indulgence swinging and it is hard to see how it can come to rest. Even when sex becomes an industrialized product, universally traded at accessible prices, the sense of transgression never ceases; it is the transgression they are trading on.

Lest we fall into Puritan moroseness, it is worth remembering that there is a benign side to all this. As historians like Daniel J. Boorstin or writers like John

Updike and Philip Roth have understood, America's sexual contradictions have their enriching aspects. Just as the British have transmuted their class obsessions into comedy and satire, America's sexual psychosis has helped forge some of its most distinctive art. Updike's expertise in the minutiae of sexual guilt owes much to his religious background. A better and more sophisticated writer than D.H. Lawrence, he has explored the Protestant conscience in its most elastic mode. In almost everything he writes the hero has sex on the brain, and spends most of the time thinking about how he can get someone into bed, even if it is only his wife.

Updike is a practicing Christian and the intricacy of the self-analysis that can be found everywhere in his prose is a refinement of the Puritan introspective tradition. But his is a modern perspective, and as an early short story, *Lifeguard,* suggests, he sees no conflict between a religious temperament and a sensual enjoyment of the world. His narrator is a student of divinity who, enthroned on his beach above the sunbathers and swimmers, has no problem reconciling his studies with a hearty appreciation of female flesh: 'Lust stuns me like the sun. You are offended that a divinity student lusts? What prigs the un-churched are. Are not our assaults on the supernatural lascivious, a kind of indecency?'[25]

America is of course far from alone in her sexual obsessions. Although English Puritanism waned in the eighteenth century, in Victorian times it made a comeback. For all their much trumpeted sexual sophistication to this day the English seem unable to throw off a kind of sniggering lubricity on anything to do with sex. America's

Protestant sexual ethic is even more rooted than in Britain. At times one is forced to conclude that the only prospect of change will be when and if the balance of the population shifts decisively in a non-Anglo-Protestant direction. Though even this assumes that Protestant sexual attitudes have not 'contaminated' the psyche of more recent immigrants, and as the world knows American culture, in the best and worst senses, can be catching.

Puritanism is America's original sexual sin, and the more she attempts to shuck it off the more hag-ridden by the past she appears. Her churchiness and her sexual obsessions are two sides of the same coin, though even a secularization of the culture would bring no guarantee of relief. The fact that a Protestant sexual pathology still lingers in Britain, a relatively irreligious country, says much for its tenacity. Such is the power of Puritan ideas that they remain lodged deep in the mind, like wounds from ancient battles, doing the Lord knows what damage, or unexploded ordinance that can erupt at any moment. For those who favour a reduced role for the church in America's politics and society the message—that sexual cultures take generations to change, and that hypocrisies and contortions can remain endemic long after their religious rationale has disappeared—is not encouraging.

In Puritanically-minded societies the cure for sexual ignorance and dysfunction can become a part of the problem. Repressive attitudes and the over-reaction against them mean that society swings from one form of abnormality to another. Sex and the erotic are aspects of human love, and a condemnatory attitude is a perversion of the human spirit. At the same time a wholly uninhibited approach is no solution. Openness is seen as 'healthy' and 'wholesome', but as America has cause to know, the results can be depressing. That is the cycle America appears to be caught up in, and for the moment there seems no escape. In America (as in England) the suppression of the bodily truths about life is a sickness in the blood, for which the cure—a raging for sexual freedom—can turn into a secondary disease. The solution is not to have the sickness.

4

HOLY BUSINESS

'The country where the cross is only a plus sign.'
                                            Paul Morand.

Everyone is familiar with Max Weber's theory about how religion gave rise to modern capitalism. Theories, however, have a habit of conflicting with common sense and the evidence before our eyes. Ever since Calvin and the English Puritans, then their American brothers advanced it, the idea that piety and profits are reconcilable in the eyes of the Lord has had something of an image problem. It certainly did to the Whig historian Lord Macaulay. Reflecting on the evolution of the stock market he wrote:

'Every day some new bubble was puffed into existence, rose buoyant, shone bright, burst, and was forgotten. The new form that covetousness had taken furnished the comic poets and satirists with an excellent subject; nor was that subject the less welcome to them because some of the most unscrupulous and most successful of the new race of gamesters were men in sad coloured clothes and lank hair, men who called cards the devil's work, men who thought it a sin and a scandal to win or lose twopence over the backgammon board. It was in the drama of Shadwell that the hypocrisy and knavery of speculators was for the first time exposed to public ridicule…The best scene [in the play] is that in which four or five stern non-conformists, clad in the full Puritan costume, after discussing the prospect for the Mousetrap Company and the Flea-killing Company, examine the question of whether the godly may lawfully hold stock in a company for bringing over Chinese rope dancers.' Their doubts about whether it would be right are settled when they decide that the performers are unlikely to come, but the shares will sell anyway.[1]

The 'race of gamesters' Macaulay holds up for our amusement are still recognizable three hundred years after he wrote these lines, which today apply more readily to America than to Britain. The characteristics of pious business folk have changed little over time. Often they are respectable and respected church-going men, and pillars of their communities. Still today they are dressed in drab-coloured clothes, even if the lank hair has been shampooed and trimmed. The bubble they spend their twelve hour days inflating may now be a media company specializing in sexually risqué but financially rewarding products, or a dot.com enterprise selling God knows what. They gamble tens of millions of dollars daily but their attitude to fruit machines (unless they operate them themselves) is likely to be similar to that of their forebears to the backgammon board.

Abstemious in their own lives, they take brief working holidays in Mexico, the Bahamas or Montego Bay, where their conversation over bad but expensive food (good food would be an indulgence) is full of laments about the drinking, drug-taking and sexual improvidence of the young and the poor. It is to minimize contact with this generation of losers that they live in gated communities, send their children to private schools, and bequeath them just enough to give them a head-start in making upstanding, self-made men of themselves, in the image of their fathers.

The feeling that capitalism and religion are in natural conflict is not new, and goes back further than Macaulay. We know from pamphlets and publications in seventeenth century England that Puritan arguments sanctifying commerce inspired incredulity and derision. Anxious not to let self-seeking drive out community values, and worried by the prospect of luxury replacing godliness, America's Puritans were not above lampooning the rapacious merchant themselves. John Winthrop, who feared that 'we would fall to embrace this present world and prosecute our carnal intentions, seeking great things for ourselves and for our posterity',[2] summed up the aims and methods of unscrupulous traders with mordant sarcasm:

1. That a man might sell as dear as he can, and buy as cheap as he can.
2. If a man might lose of casualty at sea etc in some

of his commodities, he may raise the price of the rest.

3. That he may sell as he bought, though he paid too dear etc, and though the commodity be fallen, etc.

4. That as a man may take advantage of his own skill or ability, so he may of another's ignorance and necessity.

The relevance of his squib to the less attractive face of contemporary capitalism needs little underlining.

Many early Puritans were merchants, entrepreneurs and small businessmen, so it is hardly surprising that they were often seen as hypocrites, whose arguments sanctifying commerce were as self-interested as they were convoluted. How, for example, did their money-grubbing square with St Paul's remark to Timothy, 'For the love of money is the root of all evil'? The answer seemed to be that if your riches did not lead to idleness, profligacy and luxury there was no evil involved. Yet whatever the theological justification, then or today, somehow the idea that God smiles on money-men and money-making is counter-intuitive. The fact that the driving force in the doctrine is the individual's responsibility for his own salvation, and that God takes note of those who do well in the world, makes the businessman even less of a holy figure. Sceptics will discern overtones of 'each man for himself' in his behaviour, and they would be right.

Not everyone buys the idea that it was Calvinist fear of predestination that helped drive the Protestant business type to prove himself in this world. 'Selfishness moves these men, but they call it enterprise; success rewards them, but they call it salvation, or happiness' wrote Michael Walzer about nineteenth century capitalists, though he clearly had their modern descendents in mind.[3] The Puritans, he believes, with their 'nervous lust for systematic repression and control', were more concerned with social and cultural dogma than with business ethics, and more interested in group manipulation than with individualism. 'Puritan individualism never led to any respect for privacy.'

For him Puritanism is incompatible with either liberalism or capitalism. The pretence that it is becomes justified over time, so that it ceases to be hypocrisy and evolves into an accepted way of thinking. He agrees that the emphasis they placed on methodical endeavor, trustworthiness and self-control were ideally suited to the evolution of everything from banking and commerce to Henry Ford and the conveyor belt. Essentially however their priorities lay in other directions: Walzer believes that the saints were entrepreneurs all right, but in politics rather than business.

At first sight his argument appears well-founded. The trouble arises when we see the baby disappearing with the bathwater. Social control is indeed irreconcilable with individual freedom, or for that matter with the liberty of the entrepreneur. But that does not mean that the Puritans were power-hungry cynics. What it suggests is that, in commerce as in sexual mores, their doctrinal contradictions were flagrant from the beginning, and that the legacy is there in business, sex and politics today. We cannot know what went on in these men's souls. From their behavior and most intimate confessions we must nevertheless suppose that their piety was as genuine as their self-interest—something it would be rash to assume of their godly equivalents in capitalist America today.

*

The Puritans did not invent capitalism: Chinese merchants trading in fifth century Canton, or Persians hauling their wares across the roof of the world had no need of an elaborate transcendental rationale to justify their activities. What the Puritans did for the emerging spirit of modern capitalism was to legitimize and systematize it, with their discipline, regularity and rationalistic approach. As Weber argued, the very notion of a 'calling', coupled with the peculiar personal dynamics of predestination, could be conducive to enterprise. It is true that the doctrine of personal accountability and public control on which the whole theory rested had political, as well as economic, implications. But these were not necessarily negative, and in the clash between social control and civil liberty the element of coercion did not invariably win out. '[The Puritan] drew from his idealization of personal responsibility' Tawney wrote, 'a theory of individual rights which, secularized and generalized, was to be amongst the most potent explosives that the world has known.'[4]

The Catholics' vast monasteries and sumptuous churches, with their incense and mystical communion, symbolized a striving after a spiritual life on earth. The English and American Protestants, while no less holy, were more practical-minded folk. 'God has been pleased to smile on our Merchandise and Navigation, Trade and

Business' the new Englanders announced smugly in *The People of New England Put in Mind of the Righteous Acts of the Lord, 1730.*[5] It is less easy to imagine a Catholic Bishop saying that. Puritanism answered the question of how godly men could live in a hopelessly fallen earth; the answer was in piety, but also usefully. Sloth and its concomitant, luxury, were venal sins. In America piety and business did a merger in the seventeenth century, and the basis of the deal was work. Diligence was healthy for the mind as for the soul, and if it made you rich, so much the better.

More than a means of subsistence or of self-improvement, work was a spiritual duty. Indeed such was the rigour (or perversity) of Puritan thought that they were capable of arguing that it was sometimes more godly to work than to worship. The virtuous man devotes all his time outside his religious and domestic duties to his business, but should there be any conflict piety should not invariably be the winner. Balance was everything, to the point where it could be a sin to spend too much time in prayer and too little on commercial affairs:

'For as it is a sin to nourish worldly thoughts when God sets you a work in Spiritual, hevenly employments, so it is in some respects as great a sin to suffer yourself to be distracted by spiritual thoughts when God sets you to work in civil (yet lawful) employment.'[6]

It is as if the Lord himself had said 'business is business.'

Reading their sermons on the sanctity of labour it is not hard to see why the average American puts in more hours than his Continental European counterpart, why he has

135

fewer holidays, or why his boss thinks it a sin to absent himself on long and expensive vacations when he could be making more profits. There is a side of America that is ostentatiously laid-back, though frequently the American determination to relax is combined with a constitutional inability to do so. DIY, a very Anglo-American hobby that brings together home, family, self-improvement, and work as relaxation, is a modern instance. Perry Miller suggests that the Protestant work ethic and the determination of immigrant communities to make good was ingrained from the start:

' It gave them no peace, it allowed them to make no shift with the merely good enough, it permitted no relaxation because they had done their best. English Puritanism was one of the most rigorous products of the Reformation, and those who came to New England were the most logical and consistent of the Puritans; in America, removed from the mollifying influences of an old and complex society, beginning anew where all things could be ordered not as they might like them but as God demanded and as perfection required, their rigour was proportionately intensified.'[7]

Rigour is the word. What clearer reflection can there be in modern times than the harshness of neo-liberal market economics in its American manifestation? Here is a system where success is over-rewarded, while those who do not measure up to the company's demands are summarily disposed of, along with those who do but whose services may be temporarily not required. The contrast with England still holds good. The 'old and complex society', with its inheritance of class resentment and socialist thinking, has bred more state involvement in the economy and a softer business ethos, even after Mrs Thatcher's attempt to brisk things up. In London the thoughts of someone who makes fifty million pounds will not invariably focus on the next fifty. More likely they will turn to a life of ease amidst social dignity: a draughty but noble country pile and, by dint of donations to the political party in power, a seat in the House of Lords. But it doesn't wash. In Britain financial success still carries a stigma (the kind of fellow who bought his own furniture, it was said by the would-be aristocrat Alan Clark MP of a financially successful but lesser-born colleague), even if it is fainter than before. In the end what is envied and admired is not the man who succeeds through industry and application but his opposite—the man of effortless distinction, seen as an aristocratic quality.

The contrast with Catholic France is even sharper. The Puritans would have been disbelieving at the institution by the French socialist Government of the 35 hour week. Designed to increase employment, its most obvious effect was to increase leisure. The Puritans' concerns for the moral welfare of men and women left too much to their own devices would have been vindicated by a single French statistic: a year after the 35 hour week was put into effect it was noted that there had been a steep rise in the occupancy rate of French hotel rooms. The reason turned out to be an increase in demand in the late afternoon—the moment for the *cinq à sept,* the favourite French time for illicit liaisons.

Work involved engagement with the world, as well as higher levels of comfort and prosperity, to which—within limits—the Puritans were not opposed. An ascetic, word-

137

shunning existence, with its beggarly friars and mendicant monks, was the antithesis of everything they believed in. Poverty was not a virtue: it was a sign of indolence, and what we would call inadequacy. The Puritan businessman felt no guilt in going from prayer to counting house, any more than today's corporate executive feels incongruous entering his local chapel in his weekend retreat. Nor did you stop working simply because you had attained material sufficiency. You went on toiling and accumulating because it was your duty before God to do so, and because if you stopped for a moment you might fall victim to sloth and vice. To adapt the old maxim: all work and no play make Jack a most spiritual as well as exceedingly rich boy. And if it also makes him dull, no matter: a fun-loving fellow was not what the Puritans had in mind.

Put like that theirs seems an unappealing, as well as a not especially moral way to live one's life, but the results could be beneficent to others. As in today's trickle-down theories, or in Adam Smith's idea of an invisible hand guiding the entrepreneur to help his fellow men despite himself, the drive was individual but the fruits could accrue to the general good. Ideas about the public utility of private selfishness in providing employment, economic dynamism, fiscal revenue, sources of charitable giving in the arts and sciences and so on are well ventilated in our times. The sanctimonious businessman may be an unedifying spectacle, yet it is hard to deny that the vitality of American life—its wealth-production, its science and technology, its gift of self-invention, its philanthropic culture—owe much to his example.

The Puritans did not come to America to found an

ascetic order: to live in poverty in a state of nature. Faith and economics were inextricable from the beginning. However strong their religion, the Pilgrim Fathers, and John Winthrop especially, were worldly enough to see that the colonizing of New England was a business enterprise. Money had to be raised for his Massachusetts Bay Company and the fleet of eleven ships Winthrop commanded in 1630 carried 240 cows and 60 horses along with its 700 passengers. They came for material as well as spiritual space, for land as well as religious freedom, and they prospered mightily. The consequences are with us to this day: America has its moneyed elite, and the pretensions and vulgarity that go with it, and in the England they left behind snobbery remains largely social. Neither is attractive, yet to the extent that American money-moguls can invoke their Puritan heritage, whereas the English nobleman had done nothing to earn his status, the American aristocracy of wealth is not without its spiritual dimension. Their riches are frequently the result of their own efforts, and their accumulation once enjoyed a religious sanction.

Where the analogy between seventeenth and twenty-first century commerce begins to break down is that, unlike American financial markets today, the business ethic the Puritans were advancing was not one of easy money. True virtue lay in the piling up of wealth through steady labour, and capital was to be formed by prudent accumulation and investment rather than financial coups. The 'get rich quick' mentality of the dot.com era, of hedge funds or speculation in heating oil prices or pork-belly futures, was not what they had in mind at all.

In economics we see the reverse of the Puritan tradition as we often imagine it: a religion of inhibition, prohibition and self-control. The doctrine on business was the opposite to that on sex. In carnal relations restraint was the key; in commerce activism and adventurism were encouraged. Full of sententious arguments to justify the building up of a pile of cash ('Prudence and piety were always very good friends'[8] the Puritans' incentive to a bottom-line psychology was frank and unashamed:

'If God show you a way in which you may lawfully get more than in another way (without wrong to your soul or to any other), if you refuse this, and choose the less gainful way, you cross one of the ends of your Calling, and you refuse to be God's steward.'[9]

Logically there was no limit to personal enrichment, no theological reason why a businessman should ever stop accumulating his worldly rewards. It took an English Methodist, Wesley, to sound a warning:

'I fear, wherever riches have increased, the essence of religion has decreased in the same proportion. Therefore I do not see how it is possible, in the nature of things, for any revival of true religion to continue long. But as riches increase, so will pride, anger, and love of the world in all its branches... So although the form of religion remains, the spirit is swiftly vanishing away. Is there no way to prevent this—this continual decay of pure religion?'[10]

The spirit of his words was to be echoed by the Democratic candidate William Jennings Bryan in the 1896 presidential election. It was then that he spoke his great words 'You shall not crucify mankind on a cross of gold.' And of course he lost.

*

In many cultures it is the poorest and least educated who are the most religious. Not so in the United States, where statistically at least the well-to-do tend to be more pious than the poor. 40% of those who earn more than $85,000 are weekly churchgoers—a somewhat higher figure than those on $15,000 or under. Businessmen, along with the military, are the country's most devout religious group. Indeed religion has become a business in itself, with its 1,600 Christian radio stations and tele-evangelists, not to speak of the reinvention by some churches of the system of tithes. The contrast with the liberal professions, notably the media, is stark: business people are four times more likely to be weekly churchgoers than those in the news media, and nine times as likely as those in television.[11] No such simple divergence is found in European countries, where businessmen can be as careless about the welfare of their souls as their media analogues.

Given America's peculiar legacy it is hardly surprising that the business ethic should condition the nation's life to a greater degree than in other Western nations. It follows that the responsibility of business for the flourishing or otherwise of the country's moral life, in the widest sense of the expression, is greater. To suggest that there can be a contrast between the lack of scruple of big business when to comes to boosting profits and the superficially blameless lives of the executives who run it may not be original, but in the context of their Puritanical inheritance and church-going mores the fact acquires a new poignancy.

The sober habits and moralizing temperament of many a corporate leader do not prevent them from profiting from the weaknesses of their fellow men and women, by luring them ever deeper into a soulless, consumer-driven existence, by tempting them into debt, or by sexual titillation. Branches of business that rely on the credulity, lust, avarice or plain ignorance and stupidity of their fellow men and women for their profits are too numerous to list: fast food, instant credit, and internet pornography are a few. The least one can say is that there is a mismatch between the high proportion of religious believers amongst business folk and the unremittingly materialistic culture a good deal of their activities tend to promote.

The Puritans made fewer bones about the haves and the have-nots, the losers and winners. On the contrary, they could be remarkably brutal about it: 'The great proportion of mankind are tools and implements for others to work by', rather than 'proper agents to effect anything of themselves' it was averred by a man of God three centuries ago. Today it might seem unchristian to say this quite as bluntly as William Hubbard did in 1678, yet that appears to be the spirit in which many a man of commerce approaches his workers and his customers: as tools for his enrichment.

Calvinism itself had gone even further. Should a con-temporary entrepreneur be rash enough to attempt a justi-fication for battening on the poor for personal gain, he could quote its teaching in his defence. The following passage is from *The Westminster Confession* of 1647, Calvinism's most authoritative English text, which greatly influenced the American Puritans. It distinguishes between two classes of people: 'Some men and angels are predestined unto everlasting life, and others foreordained to everlasting death.' Of the latter—the damned from birth—it is written:

'As for those wicked and ungodly men, who God as a righteous judge, for former sins doth blind and harden, from them he not only with-holdeth his grace, whereby they might have enlightened in their understandings and wrought upon in their hearts, but sometimes also withdraweth the gifts which they had, and exposeth them to such objects as their corruption makes occasion of sin; and withal gives them over to their own lusts, the temptations of the world and the power of Satan: whereby it comes to pass that they harden themselves, even under those means, which God useth for the softening of others.'

So harsh are these sentiments that many English Puritans recoiled from this aspect of Calvin's teaching. Translated into modern practice, its meaning is harsher still. What *The Westminster Confession* appears to be saying to the manufacturers of ethically challenged products or cultural detritus is that in serving up imbecilic TV or near-beer pornography to the under-classes, and thereby confirming them in their destiny as society's cast-offs, they are doing God's work in the world.

The implications become worse when you consider that the qualities that are likely to make the businessman's products attractive to the poor, the least educated and the least intellectually endowed—emotional and sexual incontinence and the lure of instant gratification—are the very opposite of the Protestant virtues of restraint and self-control; values that our corporate Christians will uphold

143

(if not always pursue) in their private lives. Morally speaking this is the equivalent of a dealer in drugs who, asked how he feels about the damage he is inflicting on his customers' lives, disclaims responsibility on the grounds that they are a bunch of losers who will never know any better, and that if he didn't satisfy their cravings someone else would.

In cold logic—and Puritan logic could be very chilly—both Calvin and the least scrupulous business folk of today have a point. If the consumers in question are hopeless profligates who will never get a grip of their lives, little harm can be done by trading on their vices. What sticks in the craw is the idea of Christians acting on the premise that some human souls are irredeemable, and profiting from the knowledge. Basing itself on Puritan habits of thought, the American business conscience appears to be able to accommodate things that, to the non-Christian or agnostic, seem deeply impure. Puritan talk about the feck-lessness of the poor can sound remarkably like the thinking of economic ultra-conservatives today, in which whole sections of society are overtly or tacitly written off. The fact that America has become a less socially mobile society than it was (according to a recent study only Britain is less meritocratic[12), and that educational oppor-tunities are becoming as widely differentiated as incomes, makes this an even less Christian attitude.

One might have thought that religious leaders would be alive to this aspect of the matter, yet Wesley's message does not appear to have got home to today's evangelicals. Many of the conservative interests who support them are as adamant in their denunciation of the permissive society as they are vigorous in their defense of market imperatives. The result is an unholy alliance between right-wing social forces and business interests. For them the slightest infraction of a market ideology is an abomination, regardless of the fact that one of its effects can be to stupefy the populace. (It is no coincidence that in the United Kingdom, a country with a comparable Protestant tradition, a similar if less virulent scenario exists.) 'Whence do merchants' profits come', Calvin asked, 'except from his own diligence and industry?' With our longer experience of capitalism in the raw we might be tempted to a more cynical reply: from insider trading, junk bonds, ignoring environmental damage, credit card institutions exploiting the improvident, and media moguls making monkeys of the undereducated masses.

The Puritans' saving grace was charity, in its monetary rather than the sentimental sense. Implicit in the doctrine of freedom to get rich was the understanding that rich folk have a duty to help the public weal. There too the New England Way has become the American Way. The Puritans might have been gratified to know that the majority of all voluntary giving goes to religious institutions, and that the money is used to relieve poverty as well as to maintain churches. They would also have been proud that Bill Gates of Microsoft, the richest man in the world is a Christian who has pledged to give away 90% of his wealth.

Even better from the Puritan standpoint, Gates' charity is not distributed as handouts but targeted at relieving disease by scientific methods (the New Englanders were keen on science). Though some charitable activities are

145

more self-interested than others. Whether they would have endorsed a system whereby tax-sheltered wealth is channelled to research institutes, think tanks, and media outlets with an eye to the political or other benefits likely to accrue to the donors, is another debate. On business matters the Puritans could be rich in sophistry, yet even they might have raised a sceptical eye at the idea of business donors describing themselves as 'venture philan-thropists', 'social entrepreneurs' or 'players in the non-profit capital markets'

*

Where does the reputation of Weber's theory, published in 1904-5, stand on its centenary? Reactions against it have proliferated as the global economy has opened up. The latest to enter the lists is Jeffrey Sachs, economic adviser to governments and to the United Nations. His new book *The End of Poverty: Economic Possibilities in Our Time* takes issue with what he sees as Weber's excessive determinism, in the sense that a culture gets the economy it deserves. Over-reliance on cultural arguments to predict economic development has two problems in his view: cultures change with circumstances, and cultural interpre-tations are often made on the basis of prejudice in the first place.

The theory collapses, he claims, when seen against the performance of actual countries. The Catholic nations of Europe were supposed to be congenitally inferior to the Protestant north in economic terms, yet Ireland has overtaken the UK in income per capita. Asian countries with Confucian values like China were assumed to be economically shackled, yet they are moving ahead fast. India's poverty and stagnation have been explained by Hindu rigidities and mysticism, though she too is progressing. And although Muslim culture is said to be unable to adapt to modernity, countries such as Malaysia and Indonesia are developing.

The odd thing about Sachs' argument is that it tends to vindicate the Weberian thesis rather than his own. Circumstances do indeed change, and cultures are modified accordingly. But that is where Sachs misses the point. It is because countries like China and India are throwing off deep-rooted inhibitions (a static, decaying Confucianism in pre-communist China, and Hindu rigidities in India) in favour of market-driven methods that they are progressing economically. 'Capital burns off the nuances in a culture', Don de Lillo wrote in *Underworld*. That is the downside. The upside is that it can also break down barriers to constructive change. Where Middle Eastern Muslim societies are at their most traditional and despotic little moves; where Islam is more liberally interpreted, as in Malaya or Indonesia, and individuals are given greater rein, social and economic advance is made.

The pattern these nascent economies tend to follow is broadly speaking the Anglo-American model, which is steeped in a particular religious tradition. That is why the world has taken to wearing blue jeans and baseball caps rather than Arab robes and wide-brimmed Hakka hats. The point is not that cultural determinants are valid for all time: it is that the stronger the culture and the greater its success, the more it is likely to prosper, and the greater the attempts to replicate it elsewhere.

Sachs' prognostications fifteen years ago about the speed with which Russia could Westernise her economy in the aftermath of the collapse of the Soviet Union proved wildly optimistic. The reason was his under-estimation of the cultural drag on economic and political development: a persistence of authoritarian attitudes and public passivity, the dominance of the security services, and a centuries-old failure to evolve an impartial legal system. This strong-arm approach has been demonstrated in a mafia-like attitude to business and in President Putin's flagrant persecution of Khodorkhovsky, the boss of the Yukos oil company who challenged his leadership. Sachs nevertheless persists in explaining Russian setbacks almost purely in mechanical terms: failure by the West to extend loans at the right moment and so on. The question he ought to have asked is how many loans would it have been wise to extend to a system capable of rigging Khodorkhovsky's trial in the way it did?

The degree to which belief in free markets remains a function of nationality says a lot about the power and persistence of cultural determinism, even within Western nations. In one camp are the Americans, the British, the Australians, the New Zealanders and the Canadians. Continental countries remain, broadly speaking, in another. Typical of Continental practice is France, where President Chirac openly proclaims 'Anglo-Saxon liberalism' to be the enemy not just of France but of all Europe. For Gaullists as well as socialists liberalism is an affront to the Community's social and economic values. Who will prevail time will show—and the French are not doing so well—but Chirac is nevertheless right to see a fundamental distinction between two cultures.

Americans do not take the capitalist road simply because, all things considered and for all its faults and excesses, it seems the most efficient, wealth-creating system. America *believes* in capitalism. Competition is sacred, and safeguarding the purity of the principle is equated with the public good. It is that which accounts for her rigorous anti-trust laws, from which no one is too mighty to escape: hence the recent case against Microsoft. In France the Microsoft case could never have been brought, if only because a company that size would have enjoyed quasi-nationalized status, which in one way or another would have given it state protection.

Even in free-market Britain (as Edward Luttwak has remarked) Bill Gates would have been Lord Gates of Microsoft, and his technical offence smoothed over. The handing down of a sentence of twenty-five years imprisonment to Bernard Ebbers, the boss of Worldcom, as a punishment for fraud is also impossible to imagine in the United Kingdom, where he would probably have got off with five years for what would have been seen as a mere 'white collar' crime. Equally doubtful is whether the case against Christies and Sothebys for rigging their commissions, which resulted in Sotheby's American chairman, Alfred Taubman, being sent to jail, would ever have been brought in Britain.

Sachs' warning against making cultural interpretations on the basis of prejudice is well taken. But considered judgments about cultures and their economic effects do not amount to prejudice. He himself is a product of a specifically American approach to economics and international affairs, which has its own assumptions. Recently he has written optimistically about Africa, comparing the pessimism about Asia in the 1960s to pessimism about the continent today: 'Africa's suffering had been put down to bad government and corruption, but in fact poor governance was as much a result of its poverty as it was a cause.'[13] He goes so far as to predict that one day Africa could be a world leader in medical research. His belief that even the poorest countries will show themselves capable of extricating themselves from abject poverty is a heartening prognosis. What is lacking is any recognition of how far the 'can-do' aspect of American culture may influence his own attitudes in an optimistic direction.

There is a limit to how far one can go in denying the obvious. When one of Dostoyevsky's heroes came up with the possibility that two and two might make five, it was suggested that he should place himself at a distance he believed to be five feet from a railway line when a train was passing, and see what happened. So it is with the influence of religion on economics. To understand the role played by the Puritan culture in the development of American capitalism it is enough to imagine the state of the US economy today if devotees of the Russian Orthodox Church had landed in New England in 1630 rather than John Winthrop, chairman of the Massachusetts Bay Company, and associates. Since then America's belief in the trinity of free trade, free markets and free competition has become so deeply rooted as to be quasi-mystical itself. The zeal with which these beliefs continue to be expounded, and the malediction that falls on anyone who dares to question them, are a reminder of their religious origins.

Not everyone sees Weber as defunct. The Harvard historian Niall Ferguson believes that the recent divergences in economic performance of Europe and America offer the best chance of vindicating the theory.[14] The numbers speak loud indeed. Not only have Americans always worked longer hours than Europeans, but for the last twenty years they have worked even more: an additional 50 hours annually. Meanwhile the working year of the French, the Germans and the Spanish actually shrank, by around 10%. (It is true that the majority of Germans are Protestant, but the influence of Calvinism in Germany is vastly smaller.) OECD figures show that in 1999 the average American worked 1,976 hours annually, while his German counterpart—seen till recently as a model of diligence—put in a mere 1,535.

In what everyone cheerfully calls our 'increasingly globalised economy' the French now work a full one-third less than the Americans. Even America's British brothers, addicts of long hours by European standards, are 12% behind. With holidays the picture is the same: the American gets two weeks, the French, Germans and Italians some 40 days. Such statistics are heavily supported by anecdotal experience. As everyone who has ever lived and worked in both France and America knows, although sandwich-snatching has begun creeping in, the fabled French one-and-a-half to two hour lunches are not a fable.

As a further boost to Weber's standing this growing divergence between Europe and America has been paralleled in a similar widening of the gap in their patterns of religious practices and beliefs. Almost twice as many Americans as Europeans now go to church once a week or more. As Ferguson suggests, the growth of evangelism in America makes it hard to explain Europe's falling away into secularism as an inevitable side-effect of rising living standards. It certainly cannot be claimed that Europeans lack the leisure to practice their religion. The fact that the trends on hours of work and religious practice are both downwards does not of course mean that they are related, yet the fact that Europeans are working and praying less at exactly the same time as Americans are praying and working more is at the very least intriguing. Something must explain these stubbornly different habits of work and worship. If it is not the influence of history and religion translated into contemporary national cultures, then it is time somebody told us what else it might be. Till then it would be premature to topple Weber from his pedestal.

*

Defenders of the free market in all its rigour would nevertheless be wise to avoid citing the early American Puritans too loudly in their defence. Freedom of enterprise they believed in, but not what the French call *le capitalisme sauvage*—the economic jungle. For the free marketeer the third biggest bogy after communism and socialism is *dirigisme*—an economy that is centrally influenced and directed, of the kind French governments tend to prefer. Yet there could sometimes be a tinge of *dirigisme* in the American Puritans' approach to business. Keen as they were on enterprise, New England was an authoritarian entity, the church took an interest in the economy, and debate over the proper extent of government involvement was there from the start. Social engineers as well as economic libertarians—another Puritan paradox—its leaders did not believe in a completely hands-off approach.

John Winthrop did not confine himself to preaching against exploitation, and the New England authorities sought to regulate wages and impose a limit on profits—though not for long. 'Those good orders were not of long continuance' lamented Edward Johnson in 1650, 'but did expire in the first golden age of this new world.' In 1639 it had been punishable to seek a profit of over 33%, and for a while there were rudimentary price controls. 'But since that time' Johnson sighed, 'the common practice of the country had made double that advance to sin.'[15]

There was even debate about the advantages of more public investment, of a kind Lord Keynes, if not Wall Street, would have approved. As in the Depression schemes were dreamt up to help small businesses and employment in times of crisis. One was for the construction of a bridge over the Charles river and other public works. This proved a step too far for sentiment at the time; the American suspicion of big government was already there. For the same reason most preferred private to public banks: 'An empty Treasury is very much our security', it was suggested, since it 'prevents many fine schemes of Arbitrary Power'[16]—a sentiment that might find favour with many a modern American businessman. Like the small disgruntled traders of the early seventeenth century today's big corporations want to be left alone to make money. They are impatient of regulation, suspicious of the providential state (each must earn his own salvation), resentful of the Government's power to raise taxes, and doubtful of its ability to spend their money wisely.

In New England the urge to interfere, irresistible in centralized governments, never went away. Later an attempt was made to regulate banks after complaints about speculators ('A gulph of misery by stock-jobbing.'[17]) The impulse for regulation showed that Puritan divines were unhappy about giving capitalism its head, even if in the end their zeal for social control lost out and the market triumphed. Once again what had begun as discipline ended as liberty, in this case freedom to make fortunes out of cod, wood, land or rum.

*

The question of credit brought out many of the Puritans' social worries. We might have expected them to oppose it on ethical and religious grounds; the Bible, after all, warned against usury. Loans encouraged the reaping of profits without work, militated against prudence, and encouraged people to spend money they had not got. The earliest Puritans in Elizabethan England had opposed usury, but by the beginning of the seventeenth century a more nuanced view prevailed. The paying of interest, it was argued, was not outlawed in principle by the scriptures, and in practice it was impossible to differentiate between interest on capital invested in business and interest on investments in land. In the end the principle was maintained by the stipulation that loans to the needy should be interest-free.

The American colonials slid swiftly down the same slope, though not without debate. The biggest was over the establishment of a banking system. This threw up moral questions about credit in terms startlingly similar to those of our own time. There were worries about 'The great extravagance of people, especially the ordinary sort, far beyond their circumstances...', and concerns about the temptation to borrow money 'to lay out for things they have no need of.' It was insisted that credit should be shortened, to discourage people from 'consuming more than they earn.'[18] In the end expediency won out over ideology; economic reality had moved on to the point where there was no alternative. 'Humane society, as now circumstanced, would sink, if all usury were impractical' the Cambridge Association decided in 1699. There seems little doubt that Church and government would take an identical view in today's America.

It is not hard to see why banking and commerce should be so highly developed in Anglo-Protestant cultures, or why credit should be seen as a desirable stimulus to trade and commerce. Less easy to explain is why the temptation to borrow excessively is not mitigated by the Protestant ethos of prudence, self-denial and self-control. Weber's idea was that Protestant (and especially Puritan) discipline would limit personal consumption and favour savings:

'Protestant asceticism works with all its force against the uninhibited enjoyment of possessions; it discourages consumption ...And if that restraint on consumption is combined with the freedom to strive for profit, the result produced will inevitably be the creation of capital through the ascetic compulsion to save.'[19]

Consumer credit in Protestant countries is now greater than anywhere in the world, and the last thing we are seeing is an 'ascetic compulsion to save.' In America since the middle of the Eighties household debt has gone from a third to three quarters of GDP. But Weber knew that there are degrees of religious devotion, and saw enough of the twentieth century to know that mass societies had their own dynamics. A visit to America convinced him that as capitalism became more aggressive the pursuit of wealth would inevitably become 'divested of its metaphysical significance.' It is not hard to imagine what he would say today.

Who are these improvident millions, saving less than they should and borrowing more than they earn 'to lay out for things they have no need of'? Many of course are middle-class people. Many more tend to be financially ignorant, or desperate folk at the lower end of society, a prey to lenders whose inducements to run up debts confront them at every turn. People, in other words, who appear unable to learn and become mere 'tools and implements for others to work by'—the others in this instance being the shareholders in banks and credit institutions.

*

It is not only in banking and commerce that the Protestant ethic has come to dominate the world. America's extraordinary development of science and technology owes much to the Puritan ethos. Like the link between business and godliness, a connection between science and religion seems counter-intuitive, though the historical facts are clear enough. Those who think of Puritanism as an obscurantist force would do well to contemplate a single statistic: that 62% of those listed as members of the London Royal Society in its first register in 1663 were Puritans. Since 1990 the number of Nobel prizes awarded to Americans has reached some 75%, with Briton and other European countries declining to less than 10% each. And though American scientists are often atheists, a surprising number have retained their Christian beliefs. Amongst them is Francis Collins, head of the human genome project and a born-again Christian.

Having squared God and business, the Puritans had little difficulty reconciling faith and science. Nothing is more typical of their pragmatic, rationalizing spirit than the way they did it. While Catholics fretted at the implications of man being dislodged from the centre of the universe by the discoveries of the telescope, and the Inquisition kept a worried eye on Galileo, the Puritans short-circuited the entire debate. Their solution to a conundrum which had tormented scientists and theologians alike was brisk and commonsensical: since the world was God–given, how could there be a conflict between God and the science with which he Himself had endowed us? To subject the natural world to systematic empirical study was a way of expressing our wonder, and of glorifying the Lord.

To us there may seem something of a sleight of hand about this rationalization, but not to them. Their views were similar to those of the great English naturalists, with whom they remained in touch from their American fastness. Francis Bacon himself was of sound Puritan stock, and to him scientific activity was to 'the glory of the Creator and the relief of man's estate.' The promise of material betterment contained in that last, elegant phrase would have particularly commended itself to New England industrialists. As in the legitimation of commerce, the spiritual and the useful were brought together, and the businesslike New England mind looked forward to improvements in agriculture, manufacturing and navigation, as more evidence of God's bounty. The benefits of this validation of science and of its economic and social advantages are still very visible in America, most notably in the Massachusetts Institute of Technology, where advanced science is combined with a high degree of entrepreneurial awareness. Here too cultural factors remain paramount. To the frustration of their governments European equivalents to MIT are lacking, largely because of a tradition whereby intellectuals decline to soil their hands with commerce.

New England leaders took a personal interest in science. In 1641 the younger John Winthrop, later to become a member of the Royal Society himself, went to London to meet luminaries such as Comenius, the father of scientific education. Already the Americans were poaching scientific talent from abroad: Winthrop invited him to establish a scientific college in Boston, but Comenius declined. In the event it was founded by Increase Mather, another godly New Englander with a scientific caste of mind, who was Harvard President from

1684-1701. Looking into a microscope in 1690 Mather discovered yet another reason to praise the Lord, seeing there 'Animals to which many Hundreds would not Aequal a Grain of Sand.'[20] In his scientific enthusiasms Mather was not only ahead of his time, he was ahead of his people. Only two years after he had peered excitedly into his magic lens the Salem witch trials erupted, a wave of hysterical superstition in which 20 innocents were hanged.

Three decades later it was to be Cotton Mather who got ahead of public opinion. Interested in science like his father, he picked up a theory that had come from Turkey, that the way to secure immunity against smallpox was to contaminate likely victims with a mild case of the disease. The story of how he succeeded in badgering a naturally sceptical public into trying out this method during a big outbreak in 1720 is a remarkable case of scientific enthusiasm triumphing over prejudice. The Puritans were adept at fusing scientific advances with religious doctrine, the better to advance both. In 1711, Increase Mather used Newton's newly discovered law of gravity in a sermon as a fanciful metaphor for self-abnegation: 'As weights raised towards heaven become lighter, so the self, if it would fly to heaven, must lessen.'[21]

These were no sophistries designed to fool the gullible: Mather believed what he was saying. If today's science-versus-creationism debate had no equivalent for the Puritans it was not simply because this was two hundred years before Darwin: such was their religious zeal that the idea that there could be any natural explanation of the origins of the world simply did not occur to them.

In the longer term there was to be no escaping the

conflicts scientific progress aroused in the minds of believers. Just as money-making led away from a chaste and frugal life, so knowledge of the natural world must eventually lead in the direction of agnosticism or secularization for many. The case of Benjamin Franklin ('a walking paradox: a hedonistic Puritan' in the words of the historian of America Hugh Brogan) is a classic of the times. Born into orthodoxy, he developed a bent for science of the most applied kind, and slid swiftly from Puritanism to deism, leaving Boston for Philadelphia, the city of brotherly love, in the process. Yet he never became an atheist.

A twentieth century echo of his story is there in the origins of Silicon valley. The tale of Robert Noyce, the engineer/scientist from the small town of Grinnell in Iowa who played a major role in the invention of transistors and then, as boss of the Intel company in California, of integrated circuits, is a modern parable bringing God, commerce and science together. Historically it is a tale of how the spirit of seventeenth century New England journeyed West. The Mid Western town had been founded by Josiah Grinnell, an enterprising minister who sold off lots together with covenants stipulating that anyone who drank on the property forfeited ownership. James Joyce's father and forefathers were Congregational ministers and their church an offshoot of that of New England.

The Intel culture he established, like that of a New England congregation, was democratic. In his determination to avoid succumbing to the pampered, top-heavy management style by then typical of East Coast business, Noyce did his share of sermonizing. Though less religious than his father he never renounced his faith, and when he was rich sloth and luxury did not take over. Work for him was not just about production and profits, it was a mission. Josiah Grinnell's pride in his town's most successful son would have been mitigated only by the fact that Noyce smoked, drank, and exchanged one wife for another.

The most important thing about this tale (familiar to Americans through the essay by Tom Wolfe in *The Right Stuff; Two Young Men Who Went West)*, is that it could have happened in no other country. If British or Continental scientists had discovered semi-conductors it is improbable that they would have hailed from a severely religious family somewhere in the sticks, or have been brought up as fervent believers themselves. Coming from relatively modest backgrounds their talents would also have been less likely to be noticed or nurtured than in the more meritocratic USA.

Nor would they have set up their own company to exploit the invention: in Britain blue skies scientific research was seen as something noble, not to be polluted by commerce, and scientists should not be put in the undignified position of seeking funding for the work from business. Its financing (in the common European view) should be undertaken by governments without asking impertinent questions, such as whether any practical use is likely to come it. And even if a British or French Noyce had been vulgar enough to take his discovery to market it is unlikely that he would have condescended to run the company himself; that sort of dirty work is best left to others. Attitudes are currently changing for the better, but the Puritan virtues of dutifulness, diligence, self-reliance, and a readiness to engage with the practical business world, coupled with a quasi-spiritual belief in the enterprise in hand, remain purer in America than in Europe. In science and technology and their exploitation by business, the results are there to be seen.

*

The characteristics of the Puritan personality cannot be isolated from one another. At its most tolerant and enlightened America's ability to combine a scientific mindset with a religious spirit can lead to a balanced outlook on life. It is when religion degenerates into moralism, and the uses to which the science and technology are put become socially or politically questionable, that problems arise. The danger is of scientific and ethical reductionism. In foreign policy Puritanical fervour married to technically advanced weaponry can produce a steely amalgam of might and right, an unmovable conviction that the United States alone holds the truth and that she alone has the means to enforce it. When this combination of power and conviction is used to win wars against tyrants and resolve disputes, the results can be beneficial to America and the world; her stalwart, well-armed resistance to German aggression in two World Wars is example enough. When it is used in dubious foreign adventures, it can blind Americans to the notion of doubt on which democracy itself is based, not to speak of the susceptibilities of other cultures.

It is when science and ethics appear to point in different

162

directions, as in the debate over stem cell research, that things get out of hand. Other countries face similar dilemmas, and there too feelings can run high. In America however the prestige of science coupled with the power of religion make the collision between them explosive. Faith-based thinking can also give the environmental debate a transcendental aspect absent in other cultures. In Europe it would be a rash spokesman for business who dared to quote the Bible in support of the depletion of the earth's resources, but in America it happens:

'And God blessed them, and God said to them: 'Be fruitful and multiply, and fill the earth and subdue it; and have dominion over the fish of the sea and over the birds of the air and over every living thing that moves upon the earth.'

The passage has a special resonance in American history, evoking the taming of the wilderness by intrepid settlers. But to go on to argue, as a high school book used in evangelical circles does, that 'The Christian knows that the potential of God is unlimited, and that there is no shortage of resources in God's earth', smacks less of godliness than of special economic pleading.[22] Had they faced environmental problems (which in their modern form they didn't), with their earthy commonsense and respect for science the Puritans might have been less literalist about Biblical interpretation, and more prudent about husbanding finite resources.

*

Irving Kristol once expressed the view that, shorn of its

moral and religious framework, the free market degenerates:

> To the degree that organized religion has decayed and the attachment to the Judeo-Christian tradition has become weaker, to that degree capitalism has become uglier and less justified.[23]

New Englanders who saw the church's power slipping from their hands in the eighteenth century must have entertained similar concerns. Today we have greater experience on the matter, and the problem with Kristol's statement emerges with greater clarity twenty years after he made it.

Organized religion has not, as he feared, decayed, in numerical terms. On the contrary the church in America is in the ascendant. Yet few would claim that the practice of capitalism has become less ugly and more justified. Nor does Kristol's remark make much sense when applied to Europe. There the Judeao-Christian tradition is indeed in decay, in every sense, and secularism is far more developed than in America. Governments have few qualms when it comes to interfering in moral and economic matters and the operations of the market are constantly chivvied and restricted. Capitalism can still take ugly forms, notably in free market Britain, but they can hardly be said to be uglier than in church-going, entrepreneurial America.

The Puritan businessman was in the habit of confessing his faults in his diary; what we do not know was whether he corrected them, or whether the act of confession was equivalent to absolution, and that once he had made a clean breast to himself of his covetousness he felt free to continue to overcharge customers or underpay workers. The same question arises in a starker form in contemporary America, where an outward respect for Christianity appears to go along with uninhibited—and sometimes insalubrious—business practice. Perhaps they are too cynical, but for non-Americans the spectacle of bosses and staff praying together before getting down to business is not only surprising, it is distasteful. The question of cant and hypocrisy is one that haunts the whole issue of the Church and business in America, and recent events are unlikely to make it go away. Put brutally, the question all this raises is simple: if Enron was still in operation during Bush's second term at the White House, would its leaders have felt it politic to instigate prayer-meetings too?

5

THE PIETIZING OF POLITICS

'History furnishes no example of a priest-ridden people maintaining a free civil government. This marks the lowest grade of ignorance, of which their political as well as religious leaders will always avail themselves for their own purposes.'

Thomas Jefferson, 1813.

Puritanism was a creed for public as well as for private life, and its contradictions are equally striking in both domains. Ambivalence between the authoritarian and democratic sides of the system was everywhere. The status of New England itself reflected this ambiguity. In theory it was a colony under British rule, yet the doggedness of its leaders, especially during the reign of the popish Charles II, saw to it that in practice they wrested a considerable degree of liberty from the motherland. Not much of this liberty was passed on to the colony's inhabitants. Ideas of government by consent were inherent in the Puritan creed, yet unlike many of the comrades they had left behind in England, they were not troubled by ideas of equality. The leaders of New England believed that God had assigned each to his station. Any sign that their brethren were straying in egalitarian directions was swiftly denounced: 'Whoever is for a parity in any society will in the issue reduce things to a heap of confusion.'[1] In the early Puritan years it is hard to discern the origins of the populist egalitarianism that distinguishes the United States from Europe today.

The chief historian of the Puritan movement in England was until recently Christopher Hill, a fine writer and master of his subject, but with an ideological row to hoe. His view was that the Puritan revolution failed in seventeenth century England, but that the 'bourgeois revolution' it engendered succeeded. The terminology is revealing. Hill ascribes to his American counterpart, the Puritan historian Perry Miller, the view that there was a similar decline and fall in New England, 'from the City on a Hill of the Pilgrim Fathers to the eighteenth century acceptance of religion as good for business and social subordination.'[2] As a summary of Miller's views and of the American experience this is heavily loaded. The English historian commits the familiar sin of transferring his class preoccupations to other cultures, a temptation that Hill— one of those British Marxist academics who supported Stalinism—was ill-equipped to resist.

As such he was no admirer of American capitalism. To him it was clearly a matter of regret that America's Puritans never developed a socialist wing, or spawned movements like the Levelers or the Diggers, radical seventeenth century sects whose speculations about common ownership of the means of production were to prove remarkably prescient. But it is no use looking at American history through an English social prism. On the nature of American Puritanism and its aftermath, de Tocqueville and the American historian Bernard Bailyn are more reliable judges. Tocqueville wrote that religion and liberty in France pulled in opposite directions, whereas in America they marched together. And Bailyn remarked: 'There were no 'classes' in colonial politics, in the sense of economic or occupational groups whose political interests were entirely stable, clear and consistent through substantial periods of time.'[3]

The truth is that, politically, the New Englanders were in a muddle. In their democratic development the American Puritans were a category to themselves, and it remains difficult to pin down their political philosophy. Social progressives in some respects, they had no time for social equality. Self-selecting elites, they eventually came to favour what we would call meritocratic self-improvement. They were against hierarchies in the church but in favour of theocratic rule, against corrupt, high-living bishops but not domineering clerics. In its early, New England years the land of liberty, equality and opportunity was ruled by a caste of dogmatic, authoritarian men who believed that God had created the social order.

Perhaps the best that can be said is that their religious dogmas and worldly practice made them a paradoxical breed of Utopian pessimists. Democrats place hope in the people, for them mankind was irredeemably fallen, yet they aspired to establish a community of saints. In real life they were neither pessimists nor Utopians but pious pragmatists, tough-minded and courageous folk whose hostile environment and utilitarian inclinations tempered their theological convictions at every step.

A regime that favoured the education of women and servants, encouraged business and science, and whose doctrines fed an appetite for personal freedom, cannot be wholly reactionary. Like twenty-first century America New Englanders could claim that, while differentials between rich and poor were great, equality of incomes was not a goal, and that compared to other countries the meaner sort enjoyed a better standard of living. And they had a point. Rapid economic development benefited all but the most poor. Compared to analogous societies infant mortality was low, and longevity high. They were better educated than the average European, and the population was highly literate.

Natural democrats, however, they were not, and in that respect the record of the early New England church is inglorious. There were no precedents for democracy in the Bible, and a divinely ordained order which excommunicated the masses and saw social hierarchies as God-given was hardly the most fertile soil for it to flourish. They had little interest in the opinions of frail and fallible men and women whose chances of entering heaven were as slight as their earthly possessions were few. Poverty being due to indolence or inadequacy there was little point in asking the poor what they thought, still less in giving them indirect powers over the executive. Indigent fishermen, farmers or wood-fellers had little potential as living saints.

Given a free hand one suspects they would have preferred an out-and-out theocracy centrally administered by the elect, but reality obliged them to introduce a measure of local democracy. In 1634 it was agreed that four 'General Courts' should be held annually, in conclaves that mirrored English parliaments. Two representatives were put forward by every town, whose function it was to confer with the Governor and vote taxes. The Governor and magistrates were therefore indirectly elected, and a Body of Liberties codifying the colony's laws was established in 1641. All this was progress, but for a while things went no further.

*

Within a mere few decades of their arrival the Puritans began to understand that liberty in America had its inexorable dynamic. Their closed society was going to have to open up. The first great compromise with reality came when they began to get it into their heads that their community of saints was in danger of going to the devil. The immediate reason was immigration. Towards the end of the seventeenth century the realization dawned that they were going to have to live alongside lesser people than themselves, in the form of a wave of impious, low-class Englishmen, socially and intellectually a world away from those high-minded zealots, the Pilgrim Fathers. Mostly they were simple folk who took ship to New England for no more elevated reason than that they were looking for land or work, and in the eyes of the established settlers their attitudes and manners left a lot to be desired.

Fears that their society risked being grievously contaminated by baser human material began early: 'Our thoughts and feares grow very sad to see such multitudes of idle and profane young men, servants and others, with whome we must leave our children, for whose sake and safety we came over' sighed John Humfrey to John Winthrop in 1630. Before long folk like these amounted to some four fifths of the population, and Humfrey's lament was destined to become the first of many. Today it puts us in mind of a middle class couple troubled by the personal habits of their immigrant nanny/cook/gardener. The problem was that the country needed them, and domestic and economic necessity tended to win out, then as now, over their worries. If the 'profane young men' did not do the humbler work, who would?

Hard, inflexible men when they could get away with it, the Puritans had a genius for adapting to the inevitable. Eager disputants but reluctant ideologues, in the end their pragmatism overcame their theological dogmas and social qualms. Religion was becoming increasingly out of kilter with reality. Economic growth and a caste mentality did not go together. New England was filling up with folk of the humbler sort, and there could be no ignoring their needs. As the population mounted and the economy flourished the anti-democratic dogma of the saved and the damned was first compromised and diluted, then quietly overlooked.

Its logic was proving increasingly hard to apply in real life. How were individuals to behave in the face of this awesome uncertainty hanging over their lives, which in theory they could do nothing about? The most they could do was to orientate their souls to receive the Lord, like satellite dishes scanning the heavens, in the hope of establishing contact. Though you could never be certain whether or not contact had been made. Predestination also risked becoming a recipe for idleness and hedonism. If you were not amongst the elect, and like most of the colony excluded from church membership and due for damnation no matter what, why go to the trouble and inconvenience of virtuous living? And should you be destined for salvation, the same question applied: if grace was guaranteed you could afford to cut a dash while you had the time. In a world composed of the elect and the damned, in which the Lord declined to indicate how you could be one and not the other, the only rational way of living would be an orgy of self-indulgence before you were consigned to the Devil, or to heaven.

In practice there were incentives to good behaviour. If no-one could be sure who was destined to be saved, they could at least act *as if* they were amongst the chosen. By conducting themselves like the sort of person destined to receive God's grace, though that did not guarantee anything of itself, they could at least persuade themselves that they were in with a chance. A contemporary analogy might be the hope of an employee of receiving a bonus. He or she might not be sure that the company had it in mind to distribute one that year, but the knowledge that it could never even consider paying out unless the employees made more profits might be a spur to greater efforts. The catch is that even if profits leapt there would still be no guarantee that you personally would benefit, and the final say would rest with the (notoriously whimsical) boss.

The tensions between abstruse religious dogma and a dynamic economy were increasingly stark. The personal and public implications of predestination were becoming too much for society to bear. The Puritans had tested the theory to breaking point, and the theory broke. The rupture came when, after torturous debate and compromise it was agreed that the damned could improve their chances by good deeds in the world. Like all quasi-totalitarian regimes they needed a formula to justify the switch of policy, and it was John Cotton who came up with it.

The new line was that God 'aimed chiefly at the manifestation of his grace and justice, above the manifestation of his power and dominion.'[4] In other words He was more concerned with fairness than with muscle-flexing. The theological sidestep was as deft as the change was huge. Responsibility for a failed or successful life was now the individual's. Providing they lived a pious and hardworking life, no one was excluded from a covenant with God after all. The political importance of this break with the past can scarcely be exaggerated. The abandonment of the elitist creed was another boost for individualism. Now that grace was something that could be earned, rather than mysteriously bestowed, the very American idea of the 'self-made man' acquired a spiritual as well as a material dimension.

*

In spirit if not in scope the move was analogous to the

freeing of the slaves, or giving the vote to women. But just as liberating slaves did not do away with racial discrimination, the idea of winners and losers never quite died. In diverse ways in democratic America the same mindset continued to work in the interests of the elite and their progeny. When it came to ensuring the welfare and prosperity of their offspring many of the assumptions held by Puritan movers and shakers boiled down to a kind of genetics in holy form. 'God has engaged himself to do good unto them when they are propagated by virtue of the covenant [of Grace]' which 'takes hold of their seed after them', it was said of the children of the chosen.[5] The Bush, Kennedy and Gore political clans, and maybe the Clintons of the future, would feel comfortable with that.

Not a few of the Puritans' ambiguities and equivocations over democracy live on in modern America. Despite the new start of the Constitution and the emergence of a popular democracy the contours of the old Puritan society are not totally unrecognizable in modern times. To outside eyes egalitarian America has always been a puzzling phenomenon. It is there in clothes, manners, speech, accents and social attitudes, where there are fewer of the subtle classifications whose decoding mechanism is part of the genetic inheritance of every Englishmen. In the same country however the distance between elite and popular modes of existence is greater than elsewhere.

America has the highest levels of productivity in the world, widespread prosperity and property ownership, and the sharpest differentials of incomes. It has the world's best universities, the most advanced science and technology, the most highly praised symphony orchestras, the liveliest and most intelligent literature and intellectual magazines, superb contemporary architecture, some of the world's richest art collections, the best cinema and TV cartoons and sitcoms—and the most debased and extensive popular culture anywhere in the Western world. (It is significant that her nearest competitor is Britain, where the economic, cultural and educational divide is almost as large.) In Puritan New England or today's Unites States the difference between the lives of the 'elect' and the others can be equally dramatic, and the hardness of heart that characterized the attitudes of the former to the latter is not unknown today.

Populism and politics are of course intricately related, as we are once again seeing in the evangelical movement. How little the style of sacerdotal invective and moral uplift differs from age to age!

'God hath delivered you from the Paw of the Lion and of the Bear, so that you have not known by woeful experience to this day, what a wicked, oppressing ruler means, nor seen one of these cruel and imperious Beasts amongst you. God hath not given us Rulers that would fleece us, that would pull the bread out of our mouthes, that would grinde our faces and break our bones, that would undermine and robe us of our Liberties, Civil and Religious, to the enslaving of this people and their children.'

Speaking some three hundred years after Urian Oakes' apology for the Puritan regime in 1673, Pat Robertson adopts a not dissimilar tone, though he prefers insect to animal metaphors, and his message is more negative:

'It is interesting that termites don't build things, and the great builders of our nation almost to a man have been Christians, because Christians have the desire to build something. He is motivated by love of man and God, so he builds. The people who have come into [our] institutions [today] are primarily termites. They are into destroying institutions that have been built by Christians, whether it is universities, governments, our own traditions, that we have…The termites are in charge now, and that is not the way it ought to be, and the time has arrived for a godly fumigation…'[6]

In America evangelical movements have tended to precede periods of political reform. The revival launched in 1734 by the Reverend Jonathan Edwards stirred men's hearts, strengthened the drive for religious liberty, and proved a prelude to the American Revolution. A century later an even more populist revival encouraged the provision of education and the reform of prisons, and helped lay the basis for the abolition of slavery. Further social and political reform was stimulated by the third period of revivalism in the 1890s. The fourth, in the 1950s and 60s, focused its crusading zeal on the imbroglio of Vietnam and the abuses of the administration.

To conclude that the new bout of revivalism is the latest in this pattern would be optimistic. Today it is harder to discern the democratic and reformist element, and the sources of America's new 'awakening' are more difficult to define. Is it a surge of moral rearmament, a retreat from the excesses of American society—pornography, abortion, the decline of the family, materialism and the rest? Have dormant fears of a spiritual vacuum been jolted awake by the Islamic challenge? Or is it something altogether more superficial: not a genuine upsurge of faith but a flush of sentiment, a flirtation with religiosity rather than religion, mental therapeutics with a spiritual edge? Or could it be (as Samuel Huntington suggests in his book *Who Are We*) something new: a deep rumble of discontent in defence of the Anglo-Protestant way of life in the face of the dilution of the American identity, notably by immigration? The answer would seem to be: all of these and more.

'The Government of the United States is not in any sense founded on the Christian religion.' These were the words signed by President John Adams and unanimously approved by the Senate in 1797.[7] It seems unlikely that President Bush and his supporters would endorse those sentiments today. The new wave of evangelism is indisputably reactionary, if only in the sense that it fudges the line of demarcation between church and state. By the time of the American Revolution the New England clergy had lost a good deal of its power and influence to more worldly authorities. For them as for others the end of the old order was the establishment of a wall of separation between faith and politics written into the constitution, precluding the federal government from establishing a national religion and guaranteeing the right of every citizen to worship as he pleased. But it did not ban established churches in the states, and for a while some clung on. Symbolically, the Congregational Church in Massachusetts was the last to go, in 1833.

The separation between church and state is now under challenge. This reversion to pre-Enlightenment thinking is found not only in the mouths of Bible literalists. Stephen Mansfield, a religious writer whose views are by no means extreme, openly wonders about the wisdom of this his separation:

'This [increased secularization of the presidency] produced an odd and somewhat schizophrenic culture. Candidates for office routinely affirmed their faith in God as the most important aspect of their lives, and then all but promised to disregard that God once in office so as not to violate the separation of church and state.'[8]

The phrase 'disregarding that God' is a loaded way of putting things, but no matter. The point is that America is supposed to be a secular state. The public are no longer being asked to elect, as their representatives were in the days of the General Court in the seventeenth century, a statesman/priest as leader. Yet at moments during the 2004 election campaign supporters of George W. Bush appeared to be reverting to the state of affairs that pertained nearly four hundred years ago.

Different churches have different styles, but a good deal of the rhetoric of revivalism is saturated in Puritan violence of language and in Puritan exclusivity. This is not evidence of a lively democracy at work, in which dissent on ethical questions that divide honest men and women is natural, and where political spokesmen and pressure groups give as good as they get in national debate. It is one where some are portrayed as acting on Christian conscience, while the views of lesser folks are discounted for their failure to approach ethical matters in a religious framework.

Whenever he prays before Cabinet meetings or speaks of his religion in his Presidential capacity, Bush inches America back towards the original, seventeenth century position. When he talks about a spiritual shield that protects the country in addition to its armed forces, on one level he is merely asserting that God is on America's side. On another he is signaling a return to the old, pre-Jefferson, exclusivist language. Non-believers and agnostics, a not inconsiderable minority, are entitled to ask whether the shield of faith defends them too, or whether it is only for the righteous. And when it is stated (or implied) by the President, or those close to him, that the Bible is a primary source of inspiration for social or foreign policy, those who happen to believe in more rights for gays or freedom of abortion would be justified in enquiring whether they are being implicitly reduced to the status of what Cotton Mather called 'moral heathens'. The tone adopted by fundamentalist evangelicals, and at times by Presidential appointees, suggests that it does.

Mather's words are redolent of twenty-first century as well as seventeenth century intolerance, and the occasion he used them is worth recalling: he threw them at his opponents in a seizure of fury during a public debate on widening the franchise of the Church. In pursuit of their argument for wider membership, the Brattle Street Church in Cambridge, a base of liberal theologians, had devised a suggestive phrase: 'That which pertains to all is not valid, if some sorts have not a consent in it.'[9] They were speaking not in favour of universal suffrage—it was too early for that—but against keeping ordinary folk out of the Church. Yet the spirit was democratic and their words retain their ring.

This simple yet imposing phrase must surely remain valid in a legally secular age in which the evangelical movement seems bent on clawing back some of the church's lost prerogatives. In so doing it is constricting participation, not now in church affairs, but in democracy itself. Whenever a President or politician flourishes his or her religious conscience in the public's face as a guiding principle in earthly affairs, they are implicitly excluding millions of their fellow citizens, including those who, though Christians themselves, are opposed to the erosion of the wall of separation between church and state. Secular or religious, these people have consciences too. Asserting their right to follow them in opposing a biblical approach to ethical issues does not place them outside the moral law. Not even in Britain, where there is no written constitution and where technically an established Church continues to exist, do politicians do this.

The question is not whether those who claim to be in the 'moral majority' of Christians are right or wrong on any particular issue; it is that 'That which pertains to all is not valid, if some sorts have not a consent in it.' Christian views on policy, let alone policies of an extremist hue, have no extra validity by virtue of being Christian, except in Christian eyes. Despite its large majority of believers America remains mercifully far from a position where the majority of its citizens consent to the church being used as an ethical blunderbuss to dragoon heretics and dissenters into line. But the situation bears watching.

With a quarter of the electorate describing themselves as evangelicals, the political influence of religion in America is, by European standards, huge. Effectively it is greater than this figure suggests. The concentration of religious influence on the primary presidential process, or in establishing platforms at Republican conventions on subjects like homosexual rights or the teaching of abstinence, magnifies it greatly. It is inflated yet again whenever the President and his aides act as religious spokesmen. His habit of peppering his rhetoric with godly references and lines from hymns helps to keep his evangelical constituency happy. He comes before the people as more than a mere democratic head of state: like Puritan leaders before him he sees himself as 'elect' in a different sense. 'I believe God wants me to be President, but if that doesn't happen, OK'.[10] The presumption of the first part of the sentence is not diminished by the *non sequitur* in the second. (Doesn't God usually get what he wants?)

Such an atmosphere in the White House seems unlikely to foster rational, open-minded policy debate, if only because you are less likely to take issue with the decisions of a president whose claim to be divinely ordained is supported by some of his closest aides. Ambitious politicians and senior public officials are similarly unlikely to express scepticism, whether the matter in hand is the value of Bible reading or the origins of the universe, a subject on which the President has indicated sympathy with the creationist view.

*

'A kind of narcissism' was the verdict of Bill Kristol, publisher and editor of the *Weekly Standard*, when as Governor of Texas Bush made a public declaration of his religion, announcing in response to a question on a TV programme that for him the greatest thinker-philosopher was Jesus Christ. Raised in the Episcopal Church, Bush later became a member of the United Methodist Church. Though not formally aligned with religious conservatives, individual UMC churches have greater scope than other denominations in deciding their theological and social positions.

As Governor we are told that he had been active in his local church, as not a few politicians in America are. From there to invoking Christ as your philosophical inspiration is a big leap. (It is unkind to say it, but his claim suggests a familiarity with other thinkers and philosophers, something we are at liberty to doubt.) It might have been preferable for American democratic politics if, like Eisenhower, he had indicated his support for religion while keeping his personal convictions to himself: 'Faith is good for Americans, and I don't care what faith it is.' Or, like the Catholic Kennedy, if he had put his own faith and denomination firmly to one side: 'I believe in an America that is officially neither Catholic, Protestant nor Jewish.' Both are more in keeping with the spirit of the constitution than Bush's religious politicking.

Nor is his declaration of faith above criticism on religious grounds. The note of spiritual pride (or narcissism to use Bill Kristol's word) in the Presidential persona has continued to resound in remarks he has made since. Unlike the highly articulate Puritan leaders, Bush appears to have difficulty forming his thoughts into sentences, and glib pieties can easily take the place of considered reflection and meaningful communication. In public the impression conveyed is bad enough. When the pieties are uttered in private, the impression of narcissism is the greater. An example was a report of what he said off the record about his refusal to attack gays. In a conversation with an aide before he was elected, Bush declined to follow the advice of some of his strategists to court popularity by criticizing homosexuals. It is good to learn that, though opposed to gay marriage, he refused to campaign against homosexuals as such. Yet the reasons he gives for this scrupulosity are revealing.

'I will not kick gays because I am a sinner. How can I differentiate sin?'[11] The President, it appears, equates homosexuality with sin. His personal sinfulness consisted of a predilection for alcohol, a weakness he implicitly compares to homosexuality, forgetting that whereas the majority of homosexuals are born in that condition, no one is born drunk. In any case the idea that it would be wrong of the President to attack sin because he himself is a sinner is nonsense: if it were true the President could never deprecate drunkenness, which he has been known to do, citing his own example.

The truth about his cloyingly self-referential remark is that it was suffused with spiritual pride. All he needed to say in explication of his decision were words to the effect that it would be wrong to attack gays as gays, but bent theology leads to crooked thinking. His refusal to eat sweets so long as American troops remained in Iraq—a sacrifice risibly out of proportion to the sombreness of the situation—is a further example of infantile pietism. Along with many such comments this suggests that, while seeking to hark back to America's religious traditions, the President has scant understanding of what he invokes.

The tradition of coating politics in personal faith, life and breath to the Puritans, dies hard. Bush is not the first American President in recent times to revive it, but the culmination of a trend. Nor is it an exclusively right-wing phenomenon. Jimmy Carter was a born-again Christian. Both Reagan and Clinton spoke of the need for religion in public life, the former, one suspects, with more conviction than the latter. Sniffing the wind Al Gore, Bush's first opponent, declared himself a born-again Baptist in the course of the 2,000 campaign. And now Hillary Clinton is publicly re-discovering her religious roots.

If the trend continues Presidential candidates could one day be restricted to a select club of those who have had what the Puritans called a 'converting experience', or who make play with their Protestant faith in a way that Jefferson so laudably declined to do. Which party will risk alienating that 22% of the electorate who are of the evangelical persuasion? And what are the implications for the rights of non-Christians—most obviously Jews—to aspire to the Presidency? In this and many other respects the rise of religion in politics is not an extension of democracy, it is a limitation.

*

Political sermonizing is loudest on the Christian Right, but as religion moves deeper into political territory liberal evangelicals are getting in on the act. 40% of weekly churchgoers, it should not be forgotten, voted for John Kerry in 2004. When mainline churches become involved in politics the result can be little more than the expression

of genteel moral sentiments. A statement signed by
Church leaders on May 24 2004, in anticipation of the
presidential election, was exactly that. The Unity
Statement on Overcoming Poverty, signed by a number of
denominations, states:

'In America people who work should not be poor, but
today many are. We must ensure that all people who are
able to work have jobs where they do not labour in vain,
but have access to quality health care, decent housing, and
a living income to support their families. The future of our
country depends upon strong and stable families that can
successfully raise their children. We must also ensure that
those who are unable to work are cared for by our society.'

The significance of the statement lies in its inoffen-
siveness; its sentiments, hardly contentious, could be
applied to any nation and any society. The point at issue is
not the nature of these ideals but how they can be
implemented, which is the job of politicians. If political
parties were to issue an identical statement of common
goals, as un-costed as they are unspecific, the response
would be one of derision. In the mouths of churchmen the
same ideals take on a sacramental ring.

The Puritans had their faults, but they did not go in for
ethical grandstanding in the modern sense; as well as
laying down principles they were obliged to come up with
workable solutions. Theirs was not the luxurious
detachment of a spiritual pressure group. 'Hollow righteousness' was John Hooker's term for this attitude, and
the same criticism is pertinent today. As they hammered
out blueprints for the farming industry, for landowning,
for banking, on how to deal with drunkenness or protect

the poor, they were welding principle and practice together as the best politicians do. Hollow righteousness never helped anyone. As the Puritan John Bunyan wrote in *The Pilgrim's Progress*: 'At the day of doom men shall be judged according to their fruits. It will not be said then, did you believe? But were you doers, or talkers only?'

The same point applies to the book *God's Politics* by Jim Wallis. A leading evangelical and leftish liberal Wallis is censorious about business practice:

'The behaviour of Enron and other guilty corporate executives is a direct violation of biblical ethics; the teachings of both the Christian and Jewish faith excoriate the greed, selfishness, and cheating that have been revealed and condemn, in the harshest terms, their callous and cruel mistreatment of employees. Read your Bible.'[12]

Few would take issue with the thrust of Wallis's critique, even if his finger-wagging style and rasping tone ('Read your Bible!') are gratingly reminiscent of his theological opponents on the fundamentalist Right. There is no need to read the Bible to be outraged by the conduct of Enron's executives. Investors and employees of all religions and none excoriated them for their behaviour, their swindles evoked worldwide revulsion and concern, the secular legal system condemned them and they were duly punished. Churchmen are entitled to say what they think about the scandal, but in doing so they frequently add nothing, and Wallis' views are indistinguishable from anyone else's.

The Enron example is important because it is charac-teristic of his tendency to pronounce on current affairs from a higher ethical plane. The invocation of 'God's

Politics' in his book's title is designed to put opponents at a disadvantage before a word is uttered. How are we to disagree, with George W. Bush or with Wallis, if unlike us they are in touch with a higher, inscrutable authority? But we can, because his appeal to the gospels imposes on him a duty of honest debate he does not meet. In a democracy the only justification for clergymen usurping the role of politicians is when they elevate consideration of ethical issues in non-partisan ways, and throw new light on perplexing dilemmas. This Wallis fails to do, most strikingly on foreign policy.

When he speaks of America 'bombing Iraqi children' he is not raising the level of the debate, he is exploiting politics' most deplorable methods: that of conflating intentions and results. America has never bombed Iraqi children; some Iraqi children have died as a result of American bombing. Children died in the allied bombing of Germany in the Second World War, but no one except neo-Nazis would speak of the Allies 'bombing German children.' He is free to oppose the Iraq war, for the same reasons as millions of non-believers have also done. Yet as a man of faith he is not at liberty to resort to one of the lowest tricks of the politician's trade. And if Wallis is merely in the business of deploring the effects of war (what cynics call 'why-oh-why?' journalism) his invocation of the deity to underpin his position is as redundant as his remarks.

'The best contribution of religion' he writes, 'is precisely not to be ideologically predictable nor loyally partisan.' This would be a worthy sentiment were his book not a predictable attack on George W. Bush and the

Republican Party. On the domestic front he insists that protest is not enough and that solutions to child poverty and other social ills are urgent and essential. In particular he is opposed to the growing gap in wealth and in favour of more taxes on higher incomes to pay for such remedies as he offers.

As with Iraq he has a right to his views. From a rational, non-religious standpoint, many Americans have come to the same conclusions. Presented in the way they are however his programme is a false bill of goods. These are not God's politics, which by their nature remain inscrutable, they are Wallis's. And as anyone familiar with the scriptures will be aware, invoking the name of the Lord in vain is a grave misdemeanour. In this respect between Wallis and the Christian Right there is little to choose. His conviction that he is a vehicle for the expression of the Almighty's views on the relief of child poverty is on the same level of presumption as the fundamentalists' claim to know what the Bible would have said on abortion or stem cell research, had the scientific data been available earlier.

*

In a secular democracy churchmen have a duty to decide whether they are men of faith or politicians. As the Puritans discovered it is difficult to be both at once. The most common self-contradiction amongst liberal churchmen entering the political lists is illustrated in Wallis's book when in fine seventeenth century style he attacks the sin of self-seeking:

George Bush doesn't seem to grasp that the tree of
the American economy is rooted in the toxic soil of
unbridled materialism, a culture that extols greed, a
false standard of values that puts short-term profits
over societal health, and a distorted calculus that
measures human worth by personal income instead
of character, integrity and generosity.

Who could argue with that? So persuasively does Wallis's
denunciation of Mammon ring that it is easy to overlook a
sentence that appears on the next page: 'The great crisis of
American democracy today is the division of wealth.'
That too may well be true. Alternatively there may be
greater crises, perhaps of a moral or cultural nature. What
is certain is that you cannot complain that economic self-
seeking in America is unbridled, and in the next breath
that the biggest problem facing the country is to decide
who gets the spoils the ungodly capitalists have created.
What self-respecting person would wish to benefit from
poisoned fruits, grown in 'the toxic soil of unbridled
materialism'? The Puritans too thundered against luxury,
but at least they were consistent. There was nothing wrong
with turning a profit, they believed, especially since self-
seeking business activity could be to the advantage of all.
Wallis once taught at the Harvard Divinity School, an
establishment founded in Puritan times by merchants'
money.

What does all this show? That on both sides of the
political line religion in America is in danger of assuming
that most immoral of conditions, power without responsi-

bility. A cross and a surplus are no dispensation from rational debate on Left or Right. If churchmen are going to become involved in politics they lay themselves open to being judged by political criteria, which means they must abandon their immunity from hard questions. In radio or TV interviews they must be pressed on the detail of their economic strategies in the same way as politicians, and on international affairs they must acknowledge the limits of any American government to control events beyond its shores, along with its primary duty to ensure the country's security, by force if necessary. Otherwise what we are seeing is an abuse of moral authority by people whose function it is to know better, yet who choose to afford themselves the luxury of purely declaratory positions. It is little use heralding or deploring the invasion of Iraq, or calling for higher or lower taxes, without producing hard and fast policies. Then the public can see whether the sums can be made to add up, or whether peace and security are more likely to be achieved by the forceful policies advanced by the Christian Right, the more passive strategies favoured on the evangelical left, or by something in between. In foreign or domestic policy no arguments have sanctified status.

American evangelicals appear nostalgic for the pre-Enlightenment age, but they are operating in the twenty first century, and their political style is frequently a mixture of the worst of the old and of the new. There is an unhealthy concordance between their thumping certitudes and the degeneration of public debate in a television era. It is not as if America were short of the pugnacious presentation of opinion, in which displays of 'sincerity' take precedence over proof and feeling over logic, without the churches adding to the decline of reason. There is an argument for capitalism and an argument for social democracy, an argument for going into Iraq and one for staying out, but no argument at all for seeking to out-moralize the opponent by dragging God into the debate.

6

ALONE WITH AMERICA

'The catastrophe of self-reliant solitude.'

Andrew Delbanco

A country's foreign policy is not something imposed on it from without, any more than an individual is the sum total of external influences. It grows from that country's territory, from its people, their experiences and their culture, and each nation has its distinctive features. In the case of America a recurring theme has been mental isolation. The point of their adopted country, as the Puritans saw it, was as a refuge from contamination by an incorrigibly sinful world. Their attitude was one of ethical aloofness, and their physical situation harsh. When the English Puritans first began plaguing the Establishment, Archbishop Richard Hooker suggested, sardonically, a solution: since they were obviously too pure to live amongst men these querulous folk would be better off in some wilderness by themselves. And so it was to happen. A howling wilderness was how early settlers spoke of New England.

The title of this chapter was Perry Miller's way of describing the condition of those left behind after some found the going too tough and sailed back to the motherland. 'Alone with America' suggests proud independence, but also isolation and self-absorption. The thinking behind Andrew Delbanco's equally evocative phrase about the catastrophe of self-reliance points in a similar direction. He finds reflections of this state of mind in America's culture, notably in a succession of fictional characters from Melville's Ahab to Scott Fitzgerald's The Great Gatsby. It is there too, unmistakably, in New World paintings: Grant Wood's gaunt 'American Gothic' couple in front of their church, Andrew Wyeth's 'Christina' stranded in an endless field, Edward Hopper's anonymous loner perched over his drink in a late night bar, or that most iconic American image, Whistler's 'Mother'. An art historian has written of these paintings:

'All are thin but strong presences, marooned in space. When we look back to the 'Mother' the feeling of isolation these images convey seems to grow chronologically more intense, more tragic. For all her loneliness, Anna Whistler has her steadfast faith. Grant Wood's couple retain the same consolation; they also have work to do. Hopper's dejected night-owls have no creed, company or purpose.'[1]

What comes across from these powerful characters and images is their moral autarky. All are alone with themselves and the infinitude of their country. At the same time they are not dejected. As well as psychological brittleness their isolation can engender the pride and defiance of a people uplifted above others. It was Melville who, in a famous passage in *The White Jacket*, suggested that America was settled by a chosen people, that she was the 'ark of the Liberties', an example to others who was doing good to the world merely by her existence.

'And let us always remember that with ourselves, almost for the first time in the existence of earth, national selfishness is unbounded philanthropy, for we cannot do a good to America but we give alms to the world.'

With this exalted estimation of itself it is hardly surprising that American patriotism should have turned out to be different from that of other nations. To foreigners the sight of the American flag flying outside people's homes is touching and arresting. In a French town or village only one private house would be adorned with the *tricolor*, indicating that it belonged to the local mayor. In Britain the cross of St George (the English flag) is most commonly found in the windows of humble homes or council flats, suggesting that the residents are super-patriots: football fans, perhaps, of a jingoistic frame of mind and an obstreperous disposition. In America, whether flown in remote homesteads, suburbia or downtown New York, the stars and stripes retain connotations of pioneering, of a standard newly planted on some inaccessible peak or outcrop. After 9/11 what it said was that we are more American than ever and we are not afraid.

But America was afraid, and the profusion of flags that sprang up over the country had something of the nature of a talisman to ward off evil. Now that the estrangement of America has gone as far as it has the gesture of flying the flag in the face of the world has come to have a touch of defiant nationalism. Rarely in modern times has America been so alone with herself.

*

One of the first dilemmas America encountered was whether to cultivate her garden or take her mission to the world. To begin with she hesitated, undecided about whether she wanted a foreign policy at all in the European sense. The United States was long resistant to the traditional concept of diplomacy. For her it was an immoral system, with its Old World fixations about balance of power, its shady half-truths, decorous evasions and unwholesome deals.

A chosen nation is in a special position in foreign affairs. An ideal as much as a country, America has always felt that her actions abroad required a moral purpose, or at least a moral cloak. At the same time, like those hard-headed New England clerics, she must deal with the world as she finds it, and in foreign policy as in personal life pietism does not exclude self-interest. This amalgam of idealism and selfishness has obvious ambiguities, and to this day America's world view has the characteristics of a 'divided soul' in the classic Puritan tradition. The result in foreign policy is an endless tension between moralism and Realpolitik.

Two famous episodes in American history, occurring within 22 years of one another, highlight this indecision.

196

In return for its insistence that the American continents should not be considered as subjects for future colonization, The Monroe Doctrine of 1823 undertook to abstain from interfering in the internal affairs of European powers. Leave us alone in our virtuous isolation and we will leave you alone too. An ethically unassailable position, it might be thought, though one that was seen as hypocritical by an uncomprehending Europe. Next, in 1845, President Andrew Jackson asserted his country's manifest destiny: that providence had ordained that the United States be an international beacon of hope and freedom.

But how could the light of liberty be spread if America opted for a policy of virtuous isolation? To the Puritan temperament morality and inaction are incompatible. To defend her interests and be of any practical use to others, might as well as right would be needed, even a touch of guile. Abstract virtue alone counts for little in a fallen world, and the sense of destiny and the means to enforce it were there from the start: the Mayflower carried saintly folk, and twelve canon.

Like the Puritan individual whose economic self-seeking and psychic self-immersion were in danger of divorcing him from the more altruistic aspects of the creed, America has long oscillated between withdrawal from and engagement with the outside world. There were reasons enough to stay aloof: the Puritans believed they had a covenant with God, whereas much of the rest of the world, in thrall to erroneous faiths, was the region of the damned. Spiritual vanity, later to be enhanced by a sense of material and technological superiority, made her uninterested in lesser folk, particularly those of a heterodox persuasion, to whom the Puritans did not extend the religious tolerance they had demanded for themselves. 'To hell with the lot of you' was their literal view of Popish knaves, Anglican compromisers and other recalcitrants, not excluding the Quakers in their own country. Many countries still appear to America as backward nations inhabited by people whose soul she makes intermittent attempts to save, but who frequently turn out to be beyond redemption. Chief amongst today's heretics are countries who resist conversion to democracy and the neo-liberal economic model.

America's response to her mission has frequently been uncertain. Periods of soul-saving and diplomatic fervour (President Wilson after World War I, China in the Thirties, the Marshall Plan after World War II, and Bush after 9/11) alternated with bouts of isolationism. For her allies as much as her enemies this vacillation between a view of foreign policy as an outlet for missionary zeal and the temptation to pull down the shutters on an ungrateful and intractable world has been disconcerting. All the more so since high moral principle has never excluded a pugnaciously self-seeking foreign policy. Examples of a manifest self-interest dimming or extinguishing America's beacon of hope are countless. It is enough to think of her policies in Central America and the Caribbean: the 1898 invasion of Cuba, the annexing of Puerto Rico, highhandedness and low methods in Panama. These and other examples of international rapacity have given rise to cynicism about America's claim to be the custodian of a higher mission. Nor does she escape criticism when her actions appear genuinely altruistic: at that point she is accused of an excess of activism and a domineering approach to the world.

If there is one thing America is accused of more frequently than imperialist interference it is of not interfering enough. After the Cold War grave warnings were sounded against her withdrawing into her shell. Today, as she pursues her war against terror across the globe, she is fervently enjoined to get back in. What all this means is that suspicion and confusion about US motivations have reached a point where she is damned if she does and damned if she doesn't.

An instance of the tendency of America's critics to have things both ways came after the first Gulf War of 1991. Many said that she should have marched on Baghdad and 'finished the job', rather than stand aside and watch the Shias being slaughtered in the South and allowing Saddam Hussein to reconstitute his power. The same people would without doubt have been the first to decry the appalling brutality of US forces in attacking the old men and boys who were all that was left of the Iraqi army in retreat from Kuweit, or her equally scandalous lack of foresight had diehards and terrorists put up a struggle against occupation, with the inevitable heavy loss of civilian lives. (One is reminded of the Chinese criticism of Soviet policy in Afghanistan: in Beijing's eyes the Russians were guilty of adventurism for going in, and of capitulationism for pulling out.)

Examples of America's critics having things every which way are endless. When she proved reluctant to intervene in the former Yugoslavia she was castigated for

cowardice and irresponsibility; when she bombed the
Serbs in Kosovo the complaint was that in the absence of
a readiness to commit ground troops bombing was indiscriminate and futile. And when the bombing had the
desired effect with no commitment of ground troops, and
the Serb regime was overthrown, America got no credit.
When she intervened in Somalia, only to pull out, and
failed to prevent genocide in Ruanda, again she was
accused of faint-heartedness. But when she intervened in
Afghanistan after 9/11 there were criticisms too: of the
aerial campaign (bombing would never work, it was said
again, and innocents were being slaughtered), of
involvement with unsavoury Afghan allies, of the simple-
minded belief that democracy could be imposed on a
semi-medieval people, and of pursuing a policy of pre-
emptive action.

The list goes on. No one in Europe relishes the prospect
of finding themselves within range of nuclear missiles
developed by Iran, an Islamic regime whose ruling clerics
rig elections, imprison and torture opponents and connive
in terrorism, and whose President wants to erase Israel
from the map and has visions of Muslim prophets while
addressing the United Nations. Yet if there is one thing
they dislike more than the nuclearisation of a rogue state
it is the prospect of America doing anything about it. Here
again the moral equivalence argument gets yet another
outing: if one theocracy has nuclear weapons, commentators write straight-facedly, why shouldn't another? Anti-
americanism has reached a point where it overrides self-
interest, and where the temptation to score a point against
Bush has it over the long-term security of Europe. Even

America's attempts to encourage Iranian democracy are mocked, in much the same way that Radio Free Europe, which exerted a positive influence in fostering democracy in Cold War Eastern Europe, was derided in its time.

There can be no escaping the root problem. America's claim to be unlike other countries means that her foreign policy will be judged by a different yardstick from theirs. It is normally accepted that nations pursue policies that reflect their national interests, but in the case of the United States different rules apply. The international community takes America at her word: if hers is a moral mission, it cannot be sullied with considerations of national interest. Trade is the best example. When British or French governments use such muscle as they possess to boost the prospects of national companies in international markets, they are commended for their concern to provide jobs for their citizens, for their commercial acumen and export endeavours. Should the US government help American manufacturers to conquer international markets, they are guilty of economic imperialism, pursued not by business companies but by 'global corporations'. And if the contracts result in the provision of much-needed employment in this or that rustbelt city both the company and the American government will be accused of pursuing a hidden agenda.

European nations are spared this endless questioning of their actions and motives. When Italy did a deal with fundamentalist terrorists in Iraq to free a journalist, thereby providing her captors with the money and incentive to capture and murder others, the majority of observers shrugged. A disregard of principle is what is expected of

Italian governments in general, and of Prime Minister Berlusconi in particular. If America were to act the same way there would be outrage. And when France invokes the loftiest of motives to justify her refusal to countenance an invasion of Iraq, her oil and export interests in the country, and the favoured status of the Saddam regime in French Middle Eastern policy, are rarely mentioned. We just expect French policy to be like that.

A dualistic foreign policy provokes a dual response, and the charge against America is twofold. The first is that her view of herself as a messianic nation is naïve, idealistic and irrational to a dangerous degree. Simultaneously it is alleged, frequently by the same people, that her foreign policy is dictated by a determination to impose her will on weaker countries in the pursuance of nothing more elevated than a hard-headed self-interest (in oil, markets etc). The two lines of attack come together over the Iraq invasion. Here America is accused both of criminal hegemonic ambition and of criminal ingenuousness in seeking to bring freedom to a backward culture by force of arms. It ought not to be possible to make the two indictments at once. Either Americans are misguided idealists, or they are a neo-imperialistic nation cynically exploiting its position as the lone superpower on the world stage. It is of course possible to claim that the entire American position is dishonest and hypocritical, and that talk about democracy is a mere cover for her power-seeking aims. But not even America can be simultaneously naïve and cynical.

Iraq has intensified the conflict between moralism and

Realpolitik in American policy as never before. The result is that today America finds herself once again in virtual isolation, though this time not by design.

*

Where American is similar to any other country is the extent to which domestic factors influence foreign policy. Where she is increasingly distinct from her Western allies is that religion forms part of that influence. In America, the most modern of countries, a sense of resentment against modernity is felt by millions of ordinary people, often those of the Protestant faith. Academics and commentators from Samuel Huntington to Anatol Lieven have ascribed the anxieties of Protestant, white, 'little America'—the small towns, the farming country, the lower middle class in general—to a lengthening list of concerns: loss of status, immigration and the downwards pressure on wages it can entail, disgust with the decadence of contemporary America.

They feel adrift in a post-Cold War world they have ceased to understand, a world in which America's dominance contrasts with their own sense of diminishment. The result can be a mood of resentful nationalism, which is encouraged and exploited by the evangelical movement. One phrase sums up what is happening. The rhetoric of the Christian Right includes the slogan 'taking back America'. The chauvinist, anti-immigration message is clear enough: give us back our America. By chance or by design the phrase also includes the idea of taking America back in another sense: to an older, less sex-crazed, less crime-ridden, more Puritanical culture.

To point out to such people that the origins of their grievances lie to a large extent within the Protestant creed itself would do little to soothe their rancour. Like the Puritans who worried about the implications for society's morals of an influx of the ungodly, but who needed the manpower for the colony's development, the malcontents of today are afraid of the impact on their way of life of the mass immigration that appears to them to be overrunning great swathes of their country. But these are the consequences of the market capitalism that Protestantism did much to breed. To compete with China, India and the rest, America needs its army of low-paid employees. The fact that their presence can exert a depressive effect on the salaries or environment of the least well-off is seen as unfortunate, but no more. In a neo-liberal nation, where conflicts arise between the economy and the culture, the economy tends to win. The irony is that the loss of identity Protestant America feels springs indirectly from the nature of that identity.

*

The beneficiary of this climate of introversion, fear and intolerance has until recently been George W. Bush. For all his activist foreign policy following 9/11 he began as a man of isolationist instincts. The narcissism Bill Kristol identified in his character is reflected in the insularity of his early foreign policy. Narcissists, beguiled by their self-image, have little need for points of reference beyond themselves, and that appears to have been Bush's initial attitude to abroad. Much has been made of his rocky path to the presidency: his drinking, his lack of business success, and his eventual conversion. Yet to outside eyes the single most arresting feature of his life before he was elected is the absence of any inclination to travel.

Prior to his entry into the White House in 2,000 the man whom God wanted to be President, with a mission to uphold a beacon for the world, had scarcely set foot in Europe and seen almost nothing of the Third World. It may be that, like the untrue rumour that the majority of Republicans elected to Congress in 1994 did not have passports, his provincialism has been exaggerated for electoral reasons. Nevertheless, to a non-American the mindset of a well-heeled son of the world's most powerful man, educated at Yale University and seeking to make a career in public life, who experienced little urge to see anything much of life beyond his shores, is incomprehensible. The only examples of leaders of major nations who had little or no first hand knowledge of other countries are Josef Stalin and Mao Zedong; whatever your view of Bush, hardly comparable figures.

Many Americans share his stay-at-home inclinations, and his apologists could argue (tongue in cheek one would hope) that his ignorance of the world, like his inarticulacy, were part of his appeal: one of the things that qualified him to be a truly representative president. To the extent that John Kerry's image as a cosmopolitan sophisticate did him little good in the 2004 campaign, they would seem to be right. The idea that innocence of foreign countries helps make Bush a regular guy falls, however, at the first fence. There is nothing regular about his background, his education or his leadership aspirations. Holding elevated public office while having little practical or intellectual experience of how the world works is the prerogative of royalty. And perhaps that is the explanation: we live in an age where ordinariness is the new aristocracy, and Bush has (and cultivates) many of the attributes of the common man.

In any event it is a startling thought that, presidential trips aside, the man in ultimate charge of the fate of nations has less first-hand experience of foreign countries than the average tourist. One might have thought that simple curiosity would have led him to see something of the world—the Eiffel Tower, a bull-fight, or the historic sites of his Christian beliefs. It is not as if he were a chauvinist; he does not despise non-American cultures, he just doesn't seem to see the point of them. Like the least complicated and most self-contented Americans, at bottom he appears not to understand what abroad is for. It is as if it took 9/11 to jolt him awake to the existence of a world outside the United States.

Now we have the paradoxical situation where, at precisely the moment when the need to comprehend the world they live in has increased, Americans are more reluctant to travel than ever. If it is ever to understand that they do not invariably conform to the image of spoilt, uncultivated provincials it pleases the Europeans to have of them, the world also needs to see more Americans. American journalists, artists, actors, musicians, writers, businessmen, academics, and art collectors are amongst the world's most sophisticated people, yet relative to their equivalents in other nations, even they appear to travel less.

The question arises of how a self-isolating people informs itself about what is going on outside its borders. America's great non-travelling public cannot rely on getting their overseas news from the US media. A veteran CBS correspondent[2] has argued that the absence of interest in foreign affairs by American news media, especially television, is having a deleterious effect on public debate and policy making. Anecdotal experience confirms the point. It is doubtful whether 1% of Americans can name the foreign minister of a single foreign country, its close ally the United Kingdom included. The fact that Americans are the modern world's most energetic, inventive, curiosity-driven people, famed for their entre-preneurial zeal and spirit of discovery, makes this indif-ference to foreign cultures doubly strange. Today the new frontier begins on America's borders, and this one the average American appears reluctant to cross. Journeys into space arouse more interest, perhaps because (to date) it remains empty of the strange and incomprehensible folk who people the earth.

*

It helps to understand the exceptionalism of the American religious experience to define the United States in opposition to its three most recent adversaries: the Soviet Union, communist China and Muslim fundamentalism. Like America each was inspired by messianic attitudes. Russian and Chinese communist internationalism, and now the terrorist crusade of militant Islam, promote models deemed valid for the world. Yet their religious legacies were poles apart.

Tocqueville's *Democracy in America,* written in 1833, famously foresaw America and Russia as the two great powers of the future. Less well-known is *Lettres de la Russie*, by another French aristocrat, the Marquis de Custine. Un-persuaded by de Tocqueville's message of the inevitability of democracy, he decided to write a book showing that a benevolent autocracy was possible. An unorthodox individual (he was more or less openly homosexual) Custine undertook a journey to Russia during the reign of Nicholas I to collect material. His experiences there dramatically changed his mind. 'I was going to Russia to find arguments against representative government. I return in favour of constitutions.'

Appalled by the paranoia, arbitrariness and cruelty he encountered, his book turned out to be the opposite to the one he intended. Instead of hymning an enlightened despotism he condemned a vicious autocracy. The result was the most perceptive and unsparing attack on the moral and material squalor of Russia ever penned. His most depressing conclusion was that ordinary Russians appeared not only resigned to repression, but complicit in maintaining their servile state. What shocked him most was the ubiquity of mendacity.

'It must be said that Russians of every class conspire together with wonderful mutual understanding to ensure the triumph of duplicity in their country. They have a dexterity in lying and a natural talent for falsehood, the success of which repels my sincerity as much as it strikes terror into my heart.'

Anyone who, like the author, lived in Soviet Russia will know that this is no wild generalization, and that the 'dexterity in lying' remained a characteristic of Russian society as well as its government more than a century after Custine wrote these lines. Read in conjunction with *Democracy In America,* his book is endlessly revealing about the superpowers of the future. The qualities that most distinguished the Americans from their adversaries-to-be were central to their religious legacy. The Puritan sect began as an offspring of the Protestant reformation, a radical movement that was suspicious of all authority. The Russian Orthodox Church—ignorant, backward, hieratic, mystical, unreformed—was a willing instrument of the institution of serfdom and of Czarist oppression. The American Puritan exulted in freedom and worked to secure his own salvation. The Russian surrendered his liberty and his destiny to his 'little father', the Czar. The Puritan prized education and scientific knowledge, the Orthodox Church was darkly obscurantist. In Russia priests were barely literate. A single statistic says it all: in the whole of the seventeenth century Moscow printers published a total of ten secular books.

Serfdom, like communism, was an unproductive system. Until they were freed in 1861 the average Russian worker was a landless peasant, the product of his involuntary labour going to the gentry and nobility. The consequence was fatalism and inertia, not only amongst the peasants themselves but across the whole of society. Its chronic immobilism was symbolized in Goncharov's novel *Oblomov,* about a landowner perpetually on the point of reorganizing his estate but who can never quite get out of his dressing gown. Through sheer indolence he loses his young fiancée and ends up marrying a woman servant. The fact that Stolz, the friend who urges modern farming methods on him, is half-German (his name means pride) gives the novel added piquancy. German (and implicitly Protestant) dynamism is contrasted with Slavonic sloth. Oblomov is an unlikely figure in American literature, whose anti-heroes (for example Sinclair Lewis's Babbitt) have a tendency to be over, rather than under-active in their own interest.

National cultures grounded in religion are not easily budged. Economic and political progress at the turn of the twentieth century in Russia proved to be a brief interlude between the totalitarian systems of czarism and communism. Had Mrs Thatcher, President Reagan or proselytizing free market economists (the contemporary equivalents of Stolz) found time to read *Oblomov* they might have known better than to expect Russian society to be transformed into a pluralist liberal democracy overnight. The legacy of centuries of reaction in Russia was that there was no work ethic, little law, no tradition of individual freedom. That is why communism, by which individuals are reduced to a servile state, took root there in the first place. To this day its church remains a reactionary, nationalistic force, and in its attempts to modernize itself the country takes two steps forward followed by one back.

Meanwhile it elects to the presidency a former KGB operative with an instinct for order who fosters a personality cult with echoes of Stalin and the Czars, and curtails the liberty of the press. Younger folk are accustoming themselves to freedom of enterprise but the

Russian people, who Custine feared took a perverse enjoyment in their subjection, have yet to throw off their age-old apathy and deference to authority. A civil society must be constructed from the basement up, and in Russia there are scant religious or social foundations on which to build. The fact that 56% of the population are reported to believe that *perestroika* did more harm than good, and that the average male life expectancy is 57, largely because of the traditional solace of drink, are discouraging portents.[3]

Then there is the Muslim problem. Comparisons between Protestant evangelists and Islamic militants that have become a common (and counterfeit) currency amongst commentators of an anti-American persuasion have a surface plausibility. Both involve a personal confrontation between individuals and God. Both are fundamentalists. Like Muslim radicals the Puritans (and now the Christian Right) believed in the sanctity and literalness of the revealed Word. The teachings of the Koran embraced religious, social and political life; the Puritans sought to establish a Bible-based theocracy in Massachusetts, and evangelists seek to extend the influence of religion on US policies at home and abroad. And on many sexual and social matters American evangelicals and Islamic militants have intolerance in common.

Looked at more closely these similarities become as superficial as the differences are fundamental. From loosely analogous positions for many hundreds of years the two faiths have marched in opposite directions. The intellectual and artistic peaks of Muslim civilization were in the middle ages. For centuries since it has been a culture in almost continuous decline. Turkey's advance to democracy could never have happened had she not become a secular state. Indonesians and Bangladeshis have elections but the situation in Arab countries, the heartland of Islam, remains dire. According to a report drawn up for the United Nations by Arab academics in 2002, out of the seven regions of the world Arab countries had the lowest level of freedom in terms of civil liberties, political rights and independence of the media. The position of women is equally appalling. Two thirds of the region's 65 million illiterates are women, and female life expectancy is well below average. Despite the oil riches of the region, one in five Arabs lives on less than two dollars a day. Thoughtful Arabs have ceased to use Western interference as an alibi for this catastrophic situation. The Crusades and colonialism in the Middle East alone do not explain the descending spiral of Muslim culture.

Puritans and Muslims stressed humility before God, but for the first it was an active humility, for the second passive. Whatever else can be claimed for Islam it has signally failed to provide a basis for life in the modern world. The Muslim conception of law and government shuts out both politics and civil authority, as everything is gathered into the hands of the faith. Public and private are confounded, and Sharia, the only system of justice, is laid down from above and hence immutable. Classical Islamic thinkers appear to have given scant thought to public institutions: the caliphate (the Prophet's executive, as it were) is an office which was meant to function according to generalized religious exhortations. The same could be said of the Puritans in their early days, but they soon learned (or were forced) to separate their religious and civil lives. And while American Protestantism evolved towards freedom and prosperity, Arab Muslims went in the reverse direction: from a zenith of toleration, sophistication and scientific progress into the failed states and moribund cultures littering the Middle East today.

Unlike Russia or Islamic militants, China has shown little interest in transcendental religion. Confucius and the Puritans were each concerned with regulating the affairs of this world, but that is where the comparison stops. Confucianism had no single deity, its ethos was static rather than dynamic, and its lack of concern with the world outside China legendary. The German philosopher Herder caught the essence of this inertia when he compared China to 'an embalmed mummy wrapped in silk and painted with hieroglyphs, its internal circulation that of a dormouse in its winter sleep.'[4]

Freedom of enterprise has now re-vitalized the country. The release of the commercial spirit of a billion three hundred million people while the Communist Party retains power has resulted in a giant productive machine under centralized political control. The Chinese are at liberty to enrich themselves, but nothing more. The liberty of the individual remains an alien concept, resisted by her communist rulers as much as in the distant past. In the long term lack of political freedom may prove incompatible with economic advance, as a middle class develops and begins clamoring for its rights. The sharp growth in the number of Chinese Christians—there are now thought to be more Christians than Communist Party members, eighty as against seventy millions—can be seen as an assertion of the personal over the collective. Yet with no experience of democracy and little to underpin it, political evolution could take time. Clearly there is a good deal more liberty than under Mao Zedong, but given that he is estimated to have murdered seventy million of his fellow citizens to enforce his dictatorship that is not saying much.

It would also be a mistake to believe that, in a country with even less tradition of individualism than Russia, pressure for reform encompasses the entire population. As in Russia habits of subjugation die hard. How long it will take for the country to escape its authoritarian incubus is impossible to say. China is a highly distinctive culture, and its communist/capitalist structure is without precedent. Some Americans believe that as well as being an enemy in the recent past China will be the enemy of the future. What it is safe to say is that without the moderating effects of democracy on her foreign policy, and with her legacy of resentments against the colonizing West ('remember past bitterness' was a xenophobic Maoist slogan), a rich, nationalistic China, militarily strong, could be a problem.

Amongst Chinese, Russians or Arabs who have abandoned their countries for an American way of life the dynamic effects of liberty are clearly seen. (There is less assimilation amongst Muslims in Britain or Europe, where immigrants by and large retain stronger ties to their countries of origin, along with their anti-colonialist resentments.) Released from the bonds of a debilitating national culture one human being can behave remarkably like another. Freed from obscurantism and repressive regimes, emigrants of Middle Eastern origins are often successful in the West, in business or the professions.

Russian capitalists who sprouted from nowhere after the collapse of communism are more evidence of this adaptability, even if their business ethics have more in common with those of Chicago in the thirties than with America today. And the extraordinary commercial, artistic, technological and intellectual achievements of overseas Chinese, not least in America, demonstrate how in a climate of freedom the talents of the race can flourish.

*

Foreign policy begins with security. The Puritans set store by the martial spirit, their culture had a Spartan aspect, and they were well organized. Men between sixteen and sixty were required to meet for military exercise, and competitive sports like wrestling were encouraged. The first conflicts they were involved in were religious in inspiration. King Philip's war was ostensibly to convert Indians, though the element of self-interest was strong. War aims included the annexation of Indian land, by means not worthy of a civilizing mission. Their second war was against French Quebec, and to that extent directed at 'the popish whore.' New England had scant interest in the conflict, but was keen to show itself loyal to the Protestant succession of William and Mary in England. The war was unnecessary, the New Englanders were poorly prepared for it, and the result was a humiliating defeat.

By reinforcing her sense of identity religion has played a part in America's conflicts. She is frequently attacked for her Manichean attitude to world affairs, with its danger of a polarized approach and resistance to compromise, but there have been times when a clear vision between good and evil is what was needed, and when reluctance to make moral (as distinct from moralistic) distinctions was a culpable failure. 'Lukewarmnesse is loathsome to the stomach. Therefore appear in your colours what you are, that you may be known as either saint or Devil' announced a seventeenth century divine.[5] America is at her best when confronted with international challenges whose ethical profile is clear and whose resolution brings out her quasi-religious sense of purpose. Those who smile at her bouts of Wilsonian fervour do not mock her heroism and altruism in the twentieth century's major conflicts. When drawn into World Wars One and Two, and the Cold War after that, America's combination of might and right— material power and moral commitment—made her an awesome adversary.

Post 9/11 religious factors are no longer indirect but at the centre of the struggle. As a result puritanical urges and absolutes in American policy are coming to the fore. Militant Islam sees America as the infidel who must perish, and for America Muslim fundamentalist terrorism is the new anti-Christ. This perception has wrought an abrupt change in America's international stance. In the 2,000 election Bush denounced interventionist 'nation-building', and in office he was to prove cavalier in his treatment of America's allies. Two years later America had put together coalitions to build a nation in Afghanistan and was gearing up to do the same in Iraq. (Her greatest practitioner of Realpolitik, Henry Kissinger, not surprisingly voiced a warning: 'It is also the case that an attempt to bring about in a very brief period of time the evolution that took centuries in the West is more likely to produce chaos than democracy'.[6] In the backwash of 9/11 once again America is talking of her mission to impose, by force where necessary, what the Puritans used to call 'the universal dominion of right.'

It is tempting to confect parallels with the struggle against international communism, but in the case of militant Islam Cold War analogies are of limited use. The Soviet Politburo functioned in a prudential manner where resort to violence was concerned, whereas Al Qaeda is an atavistic organization driven by irrational beliefs, for whom violence itself often appears to be the dominant goal. The closest parallel is not with Russia but with Mao Zedong. The Chinese leader sought to unite Third World countries in an anti-imperialist struggle in order to impose his brand of austere, totalitarian rule on their peoples in China's image. The new warriors of Islam seek converts to their primitive vision through death and destruction. Like Mao the terrorists care nothing for human life, or for the exterminating powers of nuclear weapons. But even Mao did not want to take the world back to a seventh century model. His ultimate concerns were those of a nation state, and of course he was not religious.

So the present conflict with terrorism is without precedent. The enemy's profile appears clear-cut, yet at the same time—because of its hidden directorate and the concealment of its troops amongst the population of many countries—ill-defined. And though there is a reservoir of sympathy for Al Qaeda in the Muslim world, and for Saddam, it is not organized into identifiable political movements, or led by one nation, in the way the tightly-knit, Soviet-led Comintern helped to finance and organize local communist parties. Neither frontal battles, as with Hitler, nor armed peace coupled with tough diplomacy, as with Stalin and Mao and their successors, are appropriate weapons.

As in the anti-communist struggle, there is no lack of critics of how America's anti-terrorist strategy is being conducted, and it is possible for honest people to disagree about Western policy in the Middle East. What alarms many of those hostile to the US approach are the evangelical overtones in the White House's presentation of the struggle. 'Cowboy' used to be the adjective of choice of critics of America's foreign policy, a word that had the merit of making Europeans look wise and sophis-ticated, even when their alternative policy was little more than a display of palms and a down-turning of the mouth. 'Crusade', a word that Bush has learned to avoid, is nev-ertheless a more correct description of his policy. In the last resort cowboys can be reasoned with. Reining in the God-struck conscience is harder.

*

Iraq is a textbook case of the dualistic American approach to foreign policy. Realpolitik was in the saddle in relations with the country during the last phase of the Cold War in the 1980s. At that point there was scant evidence of sanc-timoniousness in America's dealings with Saddam Hussein. There was no attempt to promote democracy in Iraq, where its prospects were in any case non-existent. As he has frequently been reminded, Donald Rumsfeld, Secretary of State for Defence during the invasion, had dealings with Saddam in a quite another capacity at the time. Accusations of hypocrisy are easily made but less easy to stand up in any realistic appreciation of the situation at that point in the Cold War.

Iraq was the enemy of Iran. Iraq was a secular state, whereas Iran was under extreme Islamic rule, and virulently hostile to America. The Soviet Union had occupied Afghanistan, and it was reasonable to wonder whether in doing so it had an eye on the Persian Gulf. If forced to lean to one side or the other, in terms of America's wider interests it made sense to keep a line out to Iraq. In retrospect it can be argued that this was an unsound judgment, but Presidents, unlike their critics, do not enjoy the luxury of making foreign policy in retrospect. If anyone had said in the early eighties that Afghanistan would become a base for terrorist attacks on the United States mainland, or that Iraq would invade Kuwait within a decade, on the evidence available at the time they would have been seen as crazy.

Few of course had any illusions about the nature of the Iraqi regime. (Asked by the British Foreign Secretary Lord Carrington about his attitude to the Iran/Iraq war, Henry Kissinger commented in my presence: 'Pity only one can lose.') Britain's policy of maintaining contact with Saddam's odious government was similar to America's, which is why the author had the dubious privilege, as Carrington's private secretary, of meeting Saddam in Baghdad in 1980. He wore a white suit and silver tie, smoked a vast cigar, and looked and talked like a dated Chicago gangster. To have dealings with such a man at all was a perfect example of the expediency and 'balance of power' attitudes characteristic of European diplomacy, of the kind that America had excoriated as immoral in the past.

But that was before America became the major international player, and in the case of Iraq American 'realism' more than matched that of her European mentors. Not only were there offers to sell Saddam chemical weapons; when he signaled an intention to grab Kuweit the American response appears to have been neither clear nor resolute enough to give him pause. The rest we know. The pendulum of America's attitude was destined to undergo a violent swing. From a policy of indulgence towards Saddam to his demonisation (if you can demonize a demon) was only a step.

All this took place under Ronald Reagan and George Bush Snr. The liberal charge against them was that in dealing with Iraq they took expediency too far at a time when Saddam was massacring his own people. After the invasion of the country their charge against Bush was the opposite: not that he has shown too much Realpolitik, but too much moralism—an accusation that reminds us that oscillations between the two are not confined to the American Right. Liberals have always been fierce in their denunciation of America's tendency to get mixed up with obnoxious regimes—Singman Rhee in South Korea, Ngo Din Diem in South Vietnam, a long list of South American regimes headed by Chile and General Pinochet, and in the 1980s, Saddam. Enemies of hard-faced 'realism', they want human rights to be the cornerstone of American foreign policy.

On this view America would have denounced Saddam for what he was and worked to undermine him. When the Soviet Union had gone and its putative threat to the Persian Gulf and Western oil supplies with it, and Saddam invaded Kuwait, that was what America did. For all the talk of weapons of mass destruction and their (always dubious) threat to the United States, regime change and the installation of a democratic government to replace Saddam's tyranny was the primary motivation. The claim that action was needed to prevent Saddam helping Al Qaeda rested on similarly thin evidence. The fact is that with the election of George W. Bush Republican policy on Iraq had shifted from hard-line Realpolitik to hard-line moralism.

It was at this point that liberal opinion ricocheted in the reverse direction. The imposition of democracy and human rights on Iraq by force of arms, it now claimed, was profoundly misguided, and a diversion from the primary task of the fight against terrorism after 9/11. As the post-invasion difficulties mounted it was sometimes added that the country wasn't culturally ready for democracy—an embarrassing admission if your programme involves the propagation of human rights the world over. Saddam's regime was appalling, it was argued, on the other hand it was not an Iranian-type theocracy, so he could be relied on to keep religious extremism in check, and to clamp down on Al Qaeda.

Critics of Bush advanced no serious alternative policy to deliver the Iraqis from their tormentor, or for advancing democracy. In effect what they were saying was that

America should have done nothing, and that doing nothing would have had the advantage of keeping Saddam in power, so that he could keep his eye on radical Muslims and thereby act as a check to the very real terrorist threat to the United States. The logic of their position was that America's security post 9/11 took precedence over the rights of murdered or downtrodden Iraqis. So it was that, on Iraq, conservatives went from being 'realists' to become the hard-nosed purveyors of an ethical foreign policy, while liberals were transformed into Realpoliticians. Something in America's temperament makes such fluctuations possible.

One point on which everyone is agreed, whether or not they opposed the war, is that the aftermath of the invasion was not sufficiently prepared for. Two factors stand out in this line of criticism: the over-sanguine supposition that American troops would be greeted with open arms by the Iraqi populace; and the decision to disband the Iraqi army. The important thing about these policy failures is that each was the result of a pietistic caste of mind.

To the moralist's eye the situation was simple: for all the distrust of America's Middle Eastern policies, and her support for Israel, the Iraqis, who had suffered so much under Saddam, were bound to recognize the invaders' *bona fides*. They would denounce the remnants of the old regime and the terrorists who attacked their liberators, and set about building democracy. In fact the Iraqis' reaction was predictably ambiguous. As elections have since showed, a majority seized the chance of democracy, but disliked the invasion and occupation that had made it possible. Many of them blame the Americans for the lack of security rather than the terrorists and call upon them to pull out, a step that would make the security situation worse. This of course is illogical behaviour. Sadly people tend to be like that, especially in politically undeveloped, morally bankrupt Middle Eastern nations.

One mistake can lead to another. Because the Americans would be welcomed by the populace and any opposition would be light, the existing Iraqi army, it was thought, could be disposed of and replaced at leisure. In any event the force was contaminated with the habits of brutality a dictatorial regime instils in its troops, and in need of reformation. Everyone now agrees that disbanding the army was a terrible blunder at a time when, complicit as it undoubtedly had been in Saddam's regime of terror, it was the only effective Iraqi force on offer. An untidy compromise—weeding out the worst of the officers and retraining the rest—was clearly called for. Had that been done anti-American critics would have seized the chance to attack the US for cynically using Saddam's discredited troops, but so it goes; many of them attacked her for disbanding the army too. Continuing to rely on Saddam's troops would have been far from ideal, but the most practical solution in the circumstances. Unfortunately for Iraq, and for America, the wise old saw that the best is the enemy of the good does not feature in the Puritan psyche.

Both these errors were based on a misreading—or more likely a non-reading—of a foreign culture. The blame can be spread from the CIA to the Pentagon through the State Department, but Bush was the man in charge. The decisions were never going to be easy, but a President who had never shown much interest in how foreigners think or behave was not best placed to get them right. The conviction that God had selected you to be President at this time of trial for America, and that divine providence was on your side, was similarly unlikely to be conducive to a prudent and realistic understanding of the situation.

Bush made fundamental mistakes, but Democrats and liberals also have questions to answer on Iraq and 9/11. The terror campaigns of Al Qaeda and the defiance of the United Nations by Iraq that was to lead to war were in gestation long before Bush came to power. The attack on the Twin Towers took place less than a year after he had assumed the presidency, and planning for the outrage must have been well underway before he entered the White House. Intelligence on the activities of fundamentalist cells, and on the situation in Iraq regarding weapons of mass destruction was crucial. Yet under the Clinton administration the CIA's performance in each of these fields has been shown to have been seriously lacking. Again moralistic attitudes and impulses appear to have been to blame, as a misplaced fastidiousness led to the muzzling and weakening of the CIA in the Clinton years. In yet another lunge from Realpolitik to righteousness, from a no-holds-barred approach to excessive queasiness, its resources were reduced and its operations cleaned up. In particular it was forbidden to hire agents with a criminal background.

This was an appalling error. Qualms of this kind are incompatible with the defence of the open society. For an intelligence agency to be picky about its sources of information over a potential terrorist threat is like a nightclub refusing to hire bar girls with a reputation for flirtatiousness. The result was seriously to limit the CIA's efficiency. The effect on its work in Muslim countries, where agents were in short supply, was especially severe. When the blow came America, the sole superpower with the greatest intelligence-gathering machine in the world, had no idea what was about to hit it. And when it invaded Iraq it had little notion of what was happening there—or in the case of weapons of mass destruction, not happening. The Russian intelligence service is no model, but it is impossible to imagine a similar lurch from undue license to whiter than white in the rules governing its operations. The British M16, traditionally more constrained than the CIA, is hampered by no such inhibitions in recruiting agents where it can find them. Its reaction to the curbs imposed on its American colleagues was one of disbelief.

It is a sobering thought that if Clinton and Bush had been less influenced by moralistic factors in the gathering of intelligence or in the Iraqi invasion and its aftermath, it is conceivable that 9/11 might never have happened. And if America had gone into Iraq all the same, progress in dealing with insurgents would have been immeasurably faster.

*

The circumstances are very different, but the vehemence of European criticism of Bush over Iraq recalls that directed at Woodrow Wilson at the negotiation of the Treaty of Versailles. Like Bush, Wilson was a man of God and son of the manse, whose sanctimonious style did not commend itself to Europeans. The reaction to the presentation of his fourteen points of 1918 was more than a diplomatic incident: it was a clash of cultures. This was the first time America had sent troops to fight in a European war, and Wilson gave a moral edge to the conflict and its aftermath. US entry into the war was 'to make the world safe for democracy', a world that would work 'for a universal dominion of right by such a concert of free peoples as shall bring peace and safety to all nations and make the world itself at last free.' It is hard to dispute the President's aims, but it was quite an agenda, and when it came to putting his ideals into practice during the post-war wrangling the resistance of the Europeans ranged from diplomatic backsliding to overt disdain. (It says little for European consistency over time that while Wilson was damned for naivety in seeking to set up an international body to resolve disputes, Bush is reviled for his disinclination to submit to the will of the United Nations.)

The French, it goes without saying, were the most scathing. The American President talked to the conference like Jesus Christ, it was whispered, and Clemenceau—a severe anti-clerical—called Wilson's obsession with establishing a League of Nations a mystical creed. The press took things further. To the French mind Wilson was an out-and-out Puritan, a condition bordering on insanity, and critics saw the American president as mentally afflicted, a sufferer from 'religious neurosis'. And it wasn't just the French. The Englishman J.M. Keynes saw similar signs of religiosity. For him Wilson was still a Presbyterian preacher, sermonizing a conference in the belief that it was a congregation. Even Sigmund Freud pronounced on the case:

'I do not know how to avoid the conclusion that a man who is capable of taking the illusions of religion so literally and is so sure of a special personal intimacy with the Almighty is unfitted for relations with the ordinary children of men.'[7]

What the views of J.M. Keynes and Freud would have been on George W. Bush is not difficult to imagine.

*

The challenge to American leaders today is easily stated: to calm and contain apprehensions that Europe and America are drifting inexorably apart. The way this must be done is by showing that America's world view is not another facet of American evangelism. To say that the Bush administration has failed to do this, and that the result has been an unprecedented tide of americanophobia in Europe, followed by a counter-tide of resentful nationalism in America, is to state the obvious. Faith-based politics may work at home some of the time, but faith-based diplomacy never.

7

AN ANATOMY OF ANTI-AMERICANISM

'The internationalism of imbeciles.'

Alain Minc

It was the BBC TV current affairs programme *Question Time*, but when called upon to speak the woman in the audience with the bitter, belligerent face had no questions, only certainties. The subject was American bombing in Iraq and she was unhappy—furious rather—about Tony Blair's support for President Bush. At the end of her impassioned statement she said that the reason we had to go along with anything the Americans demanded was because if we didn't they would bomb *us*. People say all kinds of things on television, especially the young. The exceptional thing about this incident was that the speaker was a grown woman and that the politically-balanced audience applauded.

It was a banal yet in its way defining moment.

Watching it you were reminded that there is a stage in the evolution of public feeling when what you say no longer has to make any sense to elicit tumultuous approval. In recent years anti-Americanism has ascended to that high plateau of irrationality. Normally such outbursts are reserved for questions on crime: the slaughter of old ladies by burglars crazed by drugs, or the murder of a child by a paedophile. Now public emotion had turned against a nation whose criminality was seen to be such that it was perfectly capable of pulverizing friends who disagreed with it. The reason people are ready to believe anything about their ally and protector is not just that they are indignant about what is happening in the Middle East; it is what they think is happening in the United States itself. As with the drugged-up burglars and paedophiles they find America's mindset incomprehensible, and they are afraid.

For some anti-Americanism is justified by American behaviour; for others, like the French writer Alain Minc, it is the 'internationalism of imbeciles.'[1] The immediate cause is Iraq yet the problem transcends politics. What we are seeing is more than a spasm of animosity that owes its origins to the election of a President Europe did not like, it is the crystallization of a tendency. Historically and psychologically the roots of disaffection run deep, and we have reached a point of alienation that forces us back to basics. Of all the dissatisfactions that feed the anti-American intifada in Europe her religious revivalism is the most fundamental.

*

The Puritan reputation was poor from the beginning. In England from the late sixteenth century the word was rarely unaccompanied by some exasperated adjective: its adherents were seen as zealous, quarrelsome, hypocritical, hotheaded, proud, and contentious. 'Opinionists', the early Puritans were sometimes called, 'precise fellows' who exercised 'a needless nicety' in their deliberations, and whose contrariness on every question 'fired his zeal to madness and distraction'. Infuriating moralists whose bony, accusing fingers intruded into every pie, from church organization to May Day celebrations and the way ordinary folk lived their lives, their niggling rectitude got people down.

George Wither, a satirist writing in 1613, was all for religious piety, though:

> If you mean our busy-headed sect,
> The hollow crew, the counterfeit elect
> Our Dogmatists and ever-wrangling spirits,
> That doe as well contemn good works as merits

Then

> They are God's foes and the Church's slander
> And though they humble be in show to many
> They are as haughty every way as any.

Haughty, over-zealous, over-busy, hot-headed, proud and hypocritical, moral braggarts who pretended to be humble but saw themselves as top dogs—'the counterfeit elect.' It is not too far from here to the European vision of

Americans today as boastful, big-headed, impetuous, imperialistic, and hypocritical as ever. The name-calling was not—and is not—one-sided. The Puritans' pietism did not prevent them from giving as good as they got, and their solemnity of disposition was equaled only by their capacity for abuse: 'Antichrist's little toes' was one of the many colorful terms they used to put their opponents down. Listening to the virulent language on evangelical Christian radio stations broadcasting in America today is a reminder that, when it comes to the excoriation of the unbeliever, there too little has changed.

Not that the Puritans minded too much about being disliked: in fact one of the things people hated about them was their habit of seeing the hostility of sinners as a tribute to their virtue. No doubt there are people in the United States who view americanophobia in a similar manner today: if the Europeans are against what we are doing it must be right. Yet in this respect, one suspects, the American temperament has softened, and the majority take no pleasure in being as disliked as they are.

America's image in outside eyes has changed drastically in recent years. Till then attitudes tended to be mixed. Admired for their energy, their industry, their technology, their enterprise, and their principled and stoic approach to the defence of freedom in two world wars, they were simultaneously suspect for the same reasons as the English Puritans in the sixteenth century. In other words people warmed to the attractive sides of the American temperament and disliked the less appealing. Now the negative has won out, decisively in their eyes, over the positive. The New World is seen as an alien world, so different from what was hoped and expected after the Second World War that people who once looked at it as their natural leader no longer know what to make of it.

Where they once envied the land of opportunity and abundance now they see a land of excess—of wealth, of debt, of corpulence, of guns, of arrogance and—where terrorism is concerned—of fear. They see a great power throwing its weight about in the world and at the same time a country tempted by isolationism and a fortress mentality, and they do not know which should worry them most. All they know for sure is that the most thrillingly modern of nations seems intent on going backwards, with ever greater differences of income, renewed executions, and an incomprehensible revival of dogmatic, old-time religion.

Even sympathetic foreigners (and a few remain) understand less than ever what makes America tick. Unanswerable questions mount in their minds, contradictions they have no means of squaring. How can America's intellectual and technological sophistication be reconciled with primitive attitudes on gun law and capital punishment? How can its creed of self-seeking be combined with its religiosity? And how can its culture be at once infantile and highly mature? Nothing coming from America seems too outlandish to believe, extremes are unsettling, and in reaching an overall verdict they are increasingly disinclined to give it the benefit of the doubt. Unable to influence America into a more moderate stance in foreign policy, and afraid where it might be taking the world, some give up trying to understand altogether and lapse into the self-righteous anti-Americanism that dominates large tracts of politics and the media, not only in Europe but throughout the world. America, for a while the object of mankind's dreams, has become a summation of its discontents.

This would matter less if it were a temporary distancing, the result of a feeling that America's struggle with terrorism had become sidetracked in other adventures, leaving us all exposed to greater danger. But the problem is deeper. America's propensity to alienate herself from international opinion was there well before the invasion of Iraq. The election of a born-again President seen as a collaborator of the Christian Right hardly helped, but it did not give rise to scepticism about where America was going; it sealed it. And when Americans re-installed him in the White House four years later, in defiance of the wishes of the world's non-voting 'electorate', the most frequent reaction was: how could they? It wasn't only the country's politicians who were out of sinc with world opinion, it was American voters too. Amongst her swelling army of enemies the re-election of George W. Bush only confirmed their longstanding view that America was a sick society, and getting sicker.

Never before has the international media been so unified and relentless in its criticism of American policies—or its bias if you prefer. Where America is concerned a sort of soft totalitarianism of opinion is in force. From Peking to London, by way of Moscow, Bonn and Paris the case against the United States is treated as proven and there is little room for cool debate. Even in Britain, seen as her most sympathetic ally, commentators and programme-makers by and large toe the line. Radio or TV journalists do not incline their programmes in an anti-American direction through malice or left-wing bias—though both can feature—but instinctively. They sense that they have the majority of the public with them and that criticism of America is what the majority want to hear. And as always giving people what they want makes them feel they are on the side of righteousness. If there is bias in the selection of TV images or in the presentation of news (gloating shots of terrorist atrocities in Iraq) it is felt to be a justified bias, the kind of bias that is present in stories about gangsters or delinquents, an ethically-based bias that needs no excuse and no explanation.

What everyone has forgotten is that the British can be as allergic to America as the French. Her identity problem may be less acute than that of France, but Britain is an ex-world power, on whose willingness to make international judgments the sun never sets, and to have America ignore their collective opinions and do things her own way is a daily affront. Though there can be compensations. The election of George W. Bush is the best thing that has happened to the British media apart from his re-election. Bush makes the British feel good about themselves. That is why when his name is mentioned in public debate you can sense a kind of moral elation, as the participants mentally sharpen their swords of righteousness, and prepare for the kill.

*

The fact that American foreign policy is criticized in allied countries is as natural as criticism in America herself. It is not evidence of anti-Americanism to say that the invasion of Iraq was a rash adventure, or that America has been far too tolerant of Israeli policies towards the Palestinians. What matter are the tone in which America is attacked and the nature of the arguments against her. And there the position is clear: when it comes to excoriating America and the Americans, outrage and derision are de rigueur and any weapon will do.

As in the Cold War, opponents of her policies in the Middle East have a tendency to resort to moral equivalence. In the early years of Soviet communism it was frequently suggested that Christianity and communism had much in common, and that apparently irreconcilable systems would no doubt come together over time. (The theory was famously disputed on the grounds that Christ preached that what's mine is thine, whereas with communism it was the other way round.) The doctrine of convergence this particular fallacy was called. As late as 1985 J.K. Galbraith was taking a similar line after a visit to Russia, whose economic progress he found reason to praise extravagantly, a mere five years before the country's complete collapse.

Today it passes for wisdom to observe that America's evangelical foreign policy and Muslim atavism share similar aims and methods. A few days after the bombings on the London Tube on 7 July 2005 the Times cartoonist Peter Brookes showed a hooded terrorist with his hand on a bomb labeled 'indiscriminate killer aimed at urban centre' alongside an American general with an identical bomb bearing the same inscription, under the rubric: 'Spot the Difference.'

It is not just cartoonists whose indictment of America goes way over the top. Otherwise sober and respected commentators have taken to claiming that America is under attack as much from within as from without. Religious conservatism in the United States, it is gravely suggested, is as hostile to the open society as Osama Bin Laden. 'If you are going to criticize monotheistic politics you don't confine it to Islam. The Christian fundamentalist Right is the most important force in the United States outside the military-industrial complex' averred the late Edward Said.[2] The equation of Muslim and Christian monotheism is as arresting in its audacity as it is fatuous in its implications. It is true that the Puritan leader Increase Mather was once called the Mahomet of New England, on account of his authoritarian style, but that was some four hundred years ago. It takes a lively imagination to see parallels between the Christian Right and a Muslim theocracy as practiced under the Taliban in Afghanistan. Campaigns to reduce abortion, promote the right to life, teach the virtues of sexual abstinence or to impose harsher penalties for criminals are hardly equivalent to a desire to impose on humanity the religious absolutism of seventh century Islam. Anti-American sentiment, however, tolerates no such nuance.

There can also be a reluctance to draw equivalences where they are more justified. The geneticist Richard Dawkins, whose anti-American opinions obtrude obsessively into his otherwise instructive books, is an example. His forté is for taking sideswipes at creationists and Bible literalists. That is his opinion and many will share it. Meanwhile militant Islam, whose atavistic irrationalism poses a rather more clear and present danger, goes frequently unmentioned by our militant atheist. Where is his scientific objectivity where the Protestant and Islamic religions are concerned? And if he feels bound to hit out at one, why not the other? The answer is clear enough, and does no honour to the geneticist, or to science.

It must be admitted that Christian as well as Muslim fundamentalists sometimes do their best to give credibility to the moral equivalence game. The suggestion by Jerry Falwell, founder of the Moral Majority Movement, that 9/11 was God's punishment for America's pagan ways, found an echo in statements by Muslim clerics, who blamed the tsunami in Indonesia on the country's tolerance of dissolute Western tourists:

'People must ask themselves why this earthquake occurred in this area and not in others. Whoever examines these areas discovers that they are tourism areas where the forbidden acts are widespread, as well as alcohol consumption, drug abuse and acts of abomination.'[3]

In France anti-Americanism is of course endemic. Traditionally it has inspired pleasurable feelings of cultural disdain; currently it helps to provide a badge of identity to a country plagued by ontological self-doubt. Sometimes French apprehensions about US policy can be justified; often the criticism tells us as much about the critics as about the United States. Quite apart from the presence or absence of weapons of mass destruction, the French had good reason to oppose the invasion of Iraq, and the regime change that followed. They enjoyed indecently close relations with Saddam Hussein, and do not take well to seeing their influence in the Middle East sidelined. (The disclosure by the US Senate's investigation into the oil-for-aid programme, that two of France's most senior diplomats—the head of the Quai d'Orsay and its representative at the United Nations—were in the pay of the Saddam regime does not sit well with the high moral tone adopted by the French Foreign Minister in the run-up to the invasion.) Beyond striking condemnatory stances however there is little the French can do. In this and other respects their hostility towards America has been described as *la rage de l'impuissance*—the rage of impotence—in a country whose citizens see themselves as going nowhere in particular, and where affectations of cultural superiority are as shaky as the French economy.

In Germany anti-Americanism is linked to a similar unease about the future. In addition there is an opting-out from hard international realities, for historical reasons too recent and too obvious to need recalling. Though Germany being Germany even her pacifism can sound aggressive, and to many the neo-fascism of contemporary America hardly needs to be proven. Discussing the German film *The Downfall*, about Hitler's dying days in his Berlin bunker, the producer, Bernd Eichinger, said something utterly extraordinary, yet in the present climate so banal that scarcely anyone noticed:

'People might say, how could you do a film like this? But these events only happened sixty years ago and we forget them at out peril. Look at the world today. Again it is divided down racial lines—Christian fundamentalists against Muslim ones. And if you read what happened in those Iraqi prisons, you see normal people within two or three weeks starting to torture other human beings. They are told someone was a bad guy and they do it, even though no one is going to shoot them if they don't. You can see how fast what happened under Hitler can happen. It's not so far away.'[4]

These are the kind of things that film folk ad-libbing about politics tend to say, though in the mouth of a German the implications are icy. No equivalence between Hitler's crimes against the Jews and those attributed to America should be ignored, if only out of honour to the Fuhrer's victims. Abu Graib was a scandal, for which American soldiers were indicted. As a matter of official Government policy Nazi Germany murdered six million Jews and an unknown number of gypsies, homosexuals and other 'degenerates'. Ostensibly the purpose of *Downfall* was to confront Germans with the reality of their guilt and retribution for Nazi crimes, but the import of Eichinger's words is the opposite. His comparison with Iraq has the effect of relativising the horror of the Holocaust. 'It could have happened anywhere' is the burden of his remarks. In Britain and France anti-Americanism is to a significant extent a channel for resentment of a country whose international power and prestige have replaced their own. In Germany it is being used as a form of national exculpation.

The European Left have even greater reason to welcome the advent of Bush to power than the international media. For them his election was doubly providential. The demise of the Soviet Union and the discrediting of socialism in general left it as an incoherent movement in search of an ideology. Now the vacuum has been filled to overflowing. In the absence of positive social programmes (Al Qaeda and authoritarian Middle Eastern regimes are models for no one) anti-Americanism is as promising a programme as any. Its disillusioned, negative and nihilistic aspects reflect the tenor of the times. There is no longer any need to provide models or solutions because anti-Americanism itself has become a way of life.

At government level something not wholly dissimilar is happening. Critics of America's foreign policy have a tendency to assume that the Europeans, with their weight of historical experience and lack of America's missionary zeal, must have solutions. Few however appear to be forthcoming. When it comes to the encouragement of democracy around the globe American policy, over-sanguine perhaps, at least has the virtue of consistency. In the Middle East especially, Europe's record is patchy and poor. Till recently the European Commissioner for External Affairs—in effect its Foreign Minister—was Chris Patten. A former Tory Minister who lost his seat in the 1993 election, he was made Governor of Hong Kong in the years leading up to its reversion to China. In that position he was loud in his demands for democracy in the Colony and, in a book he later wrote, in China itself. A critic of previous British administrations for omitting to prepare the Colony for representative government, he attributed their failure to a mixture of timidity and expediency (kow-towing to Peking, in the jargon).

As European Commissioner the champion of democracy in China was subdued to the point of inaudibility on democracy in the Middle East. The reasons, it must be assumed, were timidity and expediency. Proclaiming the right of the Chinese to democracy gains easy media applause, but it would have taken more courage than Patten possessed to propel the European Union energetically towards a forward policy on democracy in the Middle East. (In the light of UN revelations about the Syrian regime's involvement in the murder of the Lebanese Prime Minister, the record of the EU Commission's dealings with its President, the English-educated Bashar Al Assad, who is said to have personally threatened the Lebanese leader and his family with assassination, would be worth examining.)

The causes of the EU's pusillanimity are clear enough. To insist too much on democracy would be to irritate an entire region, in which Europe has important commercial interests, not to speak of the risk of compromising its strategic ambitions to be a counterweight to the American presence. The fact that the only country in the area with a serious, democratic government—Israel—was the butt of frequent criticism by Patten, made this policy of appeasement of dictatorial regimes such as that in Syria even more cowardly and inglorious. Meanwhile the Palestinian leader Yasser Arafat was indulged with aid and support, and the corruption of himself and his regime largely overlooked.

Figures such as Patten like to contrast European sagacity to America's immature activism and impatience. Pressed on how the European Union intends to pursue reform in the benighted countries of the Middle East, their response tends to be a knowing shrug. Anyone experienced in the politics of Muslim cultures (the shrug implies) understands that they are not ready for democracy. Why China, a country ruled over five thousand years by emperors, war lords and a communist dictatorship, should be ripe for representative government and Middle East countries not is a question that is never answered, not least because no-one puts it.

In foreign policy personalities matter. Seen as caricatures of religious types, there is something irresistibly comical about European and American spokesmen on foreign affairs. Patten, a Catholic who for all his criticism of the religious element in American policy has never been averse to making political play with his own faith, is famed for his unctuously smirking, prelate's style. Bush, the uptight Protestant, suffers from a stiff, hectoring manner. And in the UN General Assembly debate over Iraq the suave, articulate and articulated French Foreign Minister Dominique de Villepin was the perfect European counterpart to the earnestly dutiful Colin Powell, self-made military man. As the wave of anti-French sentiment that subsequently swept the country showed, Americans relished being catechized by Catholic France as much as the French had enjoyed being preached at by Woodrow Wilson.

Catholicism has always tended to regard itself as possessing a superior wisdom to Protestantism in the conduct of worldly affairs. This seems somewhat dubious given its recent history, notably over its collaboration with the Nazis over the treatment of the Jews. Nor is there much evidence of it in the foreign policy stances of the American Catholic Church. One can see why it might have had reservations about Bush's policies in 2003, though confidence in the realism of its views is undermined by its position on the 1991 war. At that point it declined to support the expulsion of Saddam Hussein from Kuweit, but was in favour of keeping the Iraqis out of Saudi Arabia. So much for superior wisdom.

*

Historical precedents for discord between Europe and America are not wanting. In the British case the most obvious example was between the settlers and the British crown, though the problems date back earlier, and the tensions between English and American Puritans that preceded the War of Independence were in a way more revealing. Both were radical folk, but the Americans were a little too pure for their English brethren. The two remained in contact at the beginning of the New England Way, but quarrelled in the late 1630s. The subjects of their disputes might appear arcane to us, but are nevertheless significant in modern terms. Principally they concerned forms of worship. To the Americans the English parishes were too ready to compromise on the structures of the church, notably the role of bishops; to the English their Puritan comrades appeared too rash in their innovations, and too polemical in their sermonizing style. After testy exchanges in the 1640s the Americans examined their collective conscience, and moderated their stance.

It was a pattern that was to repeat itself at many points in the history of America's foreign policy. To this day the British like to see themselves as the mother country, moderating the excess of zeal of their well-intentioned but hot-headed progeny. Examples are Harold Macmillan's avuncular interventions with President Kennedy over Cuba, Mrs Thatcher persuading President Reagan to talk to the PLO or give a lower priority to Star Wars in the 1980s, and Tony Blair inveigling President Bush to go through the motions of working with the United Nations in the run-up to the Iraq war. The fact that such intercessions make the British feel good about themselves ('our Greece to their Rome' is the usual, excruciatingly smug formulation), and that in the Suez escapade it was the Americans who poured cold water over the hot-headed British, does not wholly invalidate the point.

What critics of America appear to want is an impossible thing: a nerveless, neutralized, pacific, moderate-minded, high-taxing, welfarised, sedate, immobile, genteel America. Given her religious and cultural traditions it seems unlikely that we shall live to witness such a transformation. Or that, in its heart of hearts, Europe would wish to see it. For if such an America were miraculously to materialize, who would have the means and the resolution to lead the Western world?

*

In the Cold War the United States faced criticism of its tactics and strategy from its European allies in its handling of the Soviet threat. Yet fellow-travelling communists apart, nobody seriously wanted America to lose and the Russians and Chinese to win. And that is the difference with Iraq and the Middle East. Commenting on the virulence of anti-Americanism the Right-wing American commentator Charles Krauthammer wrote that European hostility to the US had stopped for a single day—9/11. 'Big deal' he concluded acidly. Uncharacteristically, Krauthammer was underplaying his point. For many in Europe 9/11 was not a day of abstinence, but of scarcely suppressed rejoicing. The French philosopher Jean Baudrillard wrote of 'the prodigious jubilation in seeing this global superpower destroyed...Ultimately, they [the terrorists] were the ones who did it, but we were the ones who wanted it.'[5] Baudrillard is a known provocateur, though this time he was merely telling the truth about what large numbers of people thought. At the same moment the British *The New Statesman* carried an editorial suggesting that we should moderate our horror at the atrocity, given that the majority of the victims were capitalists.

The New Statesman and Baudrillard were not alone. Millions of people across the West felt an involuntary spasm of contentment over the incineration of three thousand human beings in the Twin Towers. Such sentiments cannot be written off as the malignant fantasy of a lunatic intellectual fringe. Even mainstream opinion was often divided between Schadenfreude at the humiliation of America and pity for the victims, and the pleasure frequently had it over the pity. Some sought to make their ambiguous feelings respectable by claiming that, say what you like, you had to admire the terrorists' audacity and technical skill. Alternatively it was stated that the moment of impact of the planes on the Twin Towers carried an undeniable aesthetic charge.

Sentiments like these were remarkable for their

callousness and hypocrisy. Would the same people have expressed aesthetic pleasure at the pleasing parabola followed by Hitler's V2 rockets before they slammed into London at the end of World War II, killing tens of thousands? And to whom would it have occurred to commend the Nazis for the advanced technology and boldness of conception that undeniably went into the construction of the extermination camps for the Jews? Some may have thought it, but by and large they didn't say it, out of a sense of decency towards the victims. No such humane reserve, it seems, applies to the slaughter of our fellow democrats in America.

The truth is that Iraq is a struggle in which large swathes of European opinion, and privately some governments, do not want the Americans to come out on top. (Asked by a journalist which side he wanted to prevail in Iraq, the then French Foreign Minister and now Prime Minister Dominique de Villepin became angry and declined to say.) Many people silently welcome every reversal America suffers in its attempts to stabilize and democratize the country. Terrorists are rarely denounced for the barbarity of their attacks; instead the Americans are criticized for failing to maintain security. Disappointment when the Iraqis braved the terrorist threats to produce a credible election was palpable in many European reports. When the missionary is mocked for his naivety, it becomes important for the mockers that he makes no converts.

The conclusion is inescapable: that it is more important for European opinion to be proved right than for the Iraqis to enjoy the benefits of progress. A failure of the two elections was especially important: a fiasco would have reinforced the wisdom of their view that democracy cannot be transplanted, and generally confirmed the image of American fools rushing in where Europeans would have known better. Aspirations that the chaos will continue are most marked on the Continent, though many others share a stake in the collapse of American policy in the Middle East. For China or Russia, America's humiliation is desirable on every ground. Even in Britain hopes for a Vietnam-type debacle in Iraq, though mostly unvoiced, are widespread. For the same reasons there was a palpable sense of awkwardness when popular pressure in Lebanon forced the occupying Syrians into retreat. Suggestions that the Americans were finally getting somewhere in encouraging democracy in the Middle East were dealt with by the most obvious of media ploys: playing up unrealistic hopes of instant progress in Lebanon, only to dampen them later.

The death-wish visited by many in Europe on American policy is frequently subconscious. The inconvenience of willing America to fail is that it equates to wanting Iraqi and foreign enemies of progress and democracy to win. Since they have no alternative policies to offer, to hope for an American defeat is equivalent to tacitly taking sides with Saddam loyalists, Islamic fanatics and terrorists linked to Al Qaeda; a morally wretched position, and an example of americanophobia at its most debased. In Vietnam the consciences of those who wanted America out was salved by the assertion that, however regrettable a communist takeover of the South (and not everyone agreed that it would be so regrettable), at least it would end the war and bring order. The idea that America should withdraw and leave the Iraqis to build democracy themselves is so patently dishonest it does not bear discussion. The same is true of the notion that the United Nations would have the muscle and willpower to police the country.

To disagree with American policy is one thing, and in her Middle East policy there has been much to disagree with. To have a psychological stake in the triumph of Islamic terrorism in Iraq, or in the collapse of the democratic experiment and the reinstallation of a thuggish regime, is another. Yet America's European ill-wishers are bound by the logic of their own self–interest to pray for an American defeat. For the political, media, foreign policy and cultural elites of Western Europe the implications of anything approaching a vindication of her policy in Iraq would be more than inconvenient: it would be intolerable. The anti-Iraq war coalition embraces diplomats, arabists, businessmen with Middle Eastern ties, TV and radio presenters, editorialists, columnists, religious leaders (including the Archbishop of Canterbury), scientists, novelists, historians and academics, film stars and generals (active and retired). All share a stake in defeat. Except on the pro-American Right—a small and embattled enclave of opinion—that is why the possibility of even a modicum of success is so rarely considered.

As of today the most likely outcome in Iraq is a shakily democratic political system involving a degree of continuous turmoil and an insecure country, in which arbitrariness and illegality will at some level persist, as the government seeks to suppress terrorists and insurgents.

Inevitably it will be claimed that in terms of human rights there is little to choose between the position under Western-imposed democracy and the brutality that went before. In the last resort it is this that will save the Europeans from the ignominy of their position. Anything that can plausibly be described as an American success cannot and must not be seen to happen. The European media can be relied on to ensure that, in terms of public presentation, it will not.

The argument is not that America was right to go into Iraq, or that in the long term her policies will be vindicated in the Middle East; that is a long and separate debate. The point is that the strains imposed on the Western alliance by what is increasingly perceived as a faith-driven US foreign policy have undermined traditional reflexes of solidarity to an unprecedented degree. So much has been invested on the back of Iraq that is has transcended politics and become a civilisational matter. The conflict with America is now more than political, it is cultural. Whatever happens or fails to happen in the Middle East, Europe's self-esteem must be saved, and America's must be diminished.

This latter aim is not confined to her ill-wishers abroad: when it comes to taking the country down a peg anti-Americanism begins at home. American idealism of the Right or Left, religious or otherwise, gives rise to a peculiarly vehement style of criticism and self-accusation when these ideals are not realized. The Puritans were radical folk, and the ferocity of their imprecations against their foes could be equalled in their denunciations of one another. This violence of feeling is echoed in radical circles today, and moral fervour can be especially fierce on all sides of America's foreign policy debate.

Alongside the self-righteous nationalism of the neo-conservatives we hear cries of self-laceration for America's actions in the world, crimes for which God's punishment can never be severe enough. Faisal Devji, a history teacher at the New School in New York, has written a book in which Al Qaeda is compared to global corporations, and America described as a 'suicide state'.[6] Puritan guilt and the need for rhetorical self-chastisement will ensure Devji and critics like him a respectful hearing on university campuses and beyond.

The aggrandizement of one's sins above those of others can be a form of spiritual pride, and it is one from which America's most vehement domestic detractors appear to suffer. For them the USA is not just a powerful country that, by a mixture of accident and ill-intention, can get things wrong abroad. It is the very devil. Critics like Noam Chomsky and Gore Vidal have looked into what they see as America's putrid heart and, like seventeenth century jeremiahs, found in it the source of all human corruption.

*

In Europe anti-americanism has a venerable tradition. In the Thirties writers as varied as the French author Georges Duhamel and the George Santayana revelled in their scorn for an upstart country. For Duhamel America was bourgeois communism. Santayana thought that 'The [American] mechanized democrat has merely learnt to have the courage of his real convictions, and to laugh at all that retrospective snobbery about being cultured and refined, a scholar and a gentleman'.[7] The burgeoning of America makes it retrospectively clear just how much snobbery there was amongst her most self-contented critics.

Today the America symbolized in many minds by George W. Bush has revived the lost pleasure of looking down on the USA from a patrician height. In the past anti-Americanism was mostly on the left, occasionally on the Right. Now it has become a rallying point for everyone from unreconstructed communists and socialists through greens and pacifists to right-wing nationalists, whether Gaullists or Little Englanders. Anti-Americanism has always had a modish edge, but now fashion is turning into settled opinion, in which fear, mockery, envy and resentment are directed in equal measure at the entire American way of life.

The ambiguities of American culture make the task of the americanophobe easy, and its critics take full advantage. There are not many countries of whom you can say one thing or its opposite and be greeted with a circle of vigorously nodding heads. It matters little whether the proposition is that Americans are terrible prudes or that they have reached a *ne plus ultra* of sexual depravity. Either way heads will nod. Excoriated for her religiosity, America is also denounced as the epitome of pagan hedonism. She is the citadel of social selfishness and a country where philanthropists make colossal donations to international aid, charities, museums, the arts, and medical research. (European countries strive, with scant success, to emulate this culture of giving.) American popular culture is seen as crass and degenerate, except when it is black or radical. And if there is one thing more risible than a corpulent American it is an American gym fanatic. Finally, as everyone knows, the trouble with Americans is that they are both an undifferentiated mass and a nation of isolated individuals, whose suffocating suburban communities won't let a man alone.

In the cultural critique of America the British emerge as the most two-faced. After a long day's anti-American indulgence many a journalist, broadcaster or columnist might relax before *The Simpsons* or *The Sopranos* or a Hollywood film, or settle down to a book on science by E.O. Wilson or a novel by John Updike, Philip Roth or Don DeLillo. They see no incongruity between their daily denunciations of America and their attraction to American culture. Works of this brio are somehow disassociated from the United States, as if they were products of some other, un-American civilization, by authors and artists whose intelligence and creative capacities entitled them to be treated as honorary Europeans. The unspoken pretence is that all this excellence has nothing in common with the other America, the one they have spent much of their day deriding as conservative, populist, vulgar, and politically primitive. British commentators frequently lament the American tendency towards a Manichean simplicity in their international attitudes, yet for them America is composed of two culturally distinct tribes. They know which one they like, and draw the line between them with the same unhesitating assurance their forefathers once did on colonial maps.

Meanwhile the British strive to maintain their belief

that their own culture is thriving as never before. British TV is the best in the world, we still endeavour to persuade ourselves, even as we watch American cartoons or sitcoms in our millions. We insist that the British film industry is in permanent renaissance, but rarely watch its films; what we love, actually, is Hollywood. We talk up our contemporary fiction manfully, in the private knowledge that it does not begin to rival America's, and for that reason are careful to exclude Americans from the Booker literary prize. We say that the last thing we would want is an American style of life, while taking cheap warm holidays in Miami whenever we can or flocking across the Atlantic to buy everything New York has to offer whenever the pound/dollar exchange rate is high. We smile at American universities as glorified six forms while knowing that the best of them are superior to our own, as a new generation of British undergraduates in Harvard or Princeton are discovering.

The downgrading of America is no longer something that needs to be discussed or argued. Not long ago the BBC World Service advertised a programme about American culture. I tuned in, expecting interviews with writers, artists, scientists, architects or musicians, and hoping that for once American spokesmen would not be selected primarily on the basis of their readiness to criticize President Bush. My fears proved groundless. The series turned out to be about American popular culture, as if that was the only culture there was. It goes without saying that its influence in the world was lamented. All of it was presented in that tone of liberal patrician hauteur so perfected by the BBC on anything to do with America.

If the British and Europeans were genuinely convinced of their superiority there would be no problem. The trouble is they are not. Their reaction to America is said to be one of attraction mixed with repulsion, but things are not so simple. The attraction is real because there is plenty to attract, but the revulsion is of two kinds: the first is a genuine horror of America's crass materialism; the second is revulsion at our own sneaking attraction to it. Europeans despise and envy America and their contempt is heightened by their envy. Which leaves them, psychologically, in a tormented state.

For them Bush is the ideal president because he does away with their doubts and allows them to give rein to their prejudices. Finally they can breathe freely and dislike America heartily. Under him all ambiguities vanish, as America acquires a two-dimensional image: of a country of imperialistic wars and electric chairs and corporate crooks and religious maniacs. The pleasure of despising the stupidity of Bush is equalled only by our distrust of the brainy (and often Jewish) neo-conservatives who surround him. His foreign policy allows Europeans to wallow in nostalgia for a time when Europe decided the fate of nations and more sensible arrangements prevailed. True, it brought upon itself two world wars, and had it not been for America, it would have been submerged by Soviet Russia. But all that is beginning to seem a long time ago.

8

TOWARDS A CIVIL RELIGION

'The Americans are the falsely religious citizens of a falsely secular nation.'
Philippe Roger characterizing French views of the US

At exactly the moment when America's Puritan habits of thought are in crisis Americans are being enjoined to return to their religious roots. Old certitudes, the belief appears to be, will help resolve today's problems, but they won't: all they will do will be to confront her with the source of her conflicts. A case not just of the cure being worse than the disease, but of the cure reviving the malady.

Initially the reports of a resurgence of religion seemed exaggerated. The context was often hostility to the Republican Party, and though individual leaders like President Bush or his Attorney General John Ashcroft were clearly what the British call God-botherers,

assertions after his first election that Christian fundamentalism had taken a grip of Washington appeared overdone.
In Europe many of the same critics were simultaneously
claiming that the Administration was in the hands of a
Jewish cabal. But for those concerned by the pietizing of
American politics a breakdown of the 2004 presidential
election confirmed the worst. 42% of total votes were cast
by people who attend church more than once a week, and
went overwhelmingly to Bush. White evangelicals, or
'born-again' Christians, formed 22% of the electorate. To
the average European atheist or agnostic these were
troubling facts. To American liberals they were equally
depressing.

Seen in historical context these statistics are less
striking than they appear. Levels of religious belief in
America remained remarkably stable over most of the last
century. When a Gallup Poll in 1940 asked people whether
they had been to church last week the percentage was
40%. Some fifty years later it was much the same, and it
is only a little more today. In the early sixties some 22%
of Americans believed in the literal truth of the Bible and
described themselves as born-again, and a similar
percentage pertains forty years on. There are two ways of
looking at these figures: either you can contend that they
demonstrate that talk of a new fundamentalism has been
oversold, or you can claim that the failure of religion to
weaken its hold on American minds is precisely the
problem.

The American sociologist Andrew Greeley has an
original explanation for what is going on. Secular interests
in the media and academia, he believes, have long been

willing a decline of religious sentiment. Discovering periodically that the church is more than holding its own, in an effort to damage what they disapprove, they have tended to talk up the dangers of religion taking over politics, inhibiting science, pursuing a reactionary morality, and generally pulling the country backwards.[1]

Equally misleading, Greeley believes, is the habit of thinking of high levels of American religious belief as an aspect of American exceptionalism. Looking at things the other way round, in his view, can make better sense. Seen over the last century the big changes in the number of the faithful have been in Europe, and it is European countries who are out of step with the rest of the world. For around a quarter of a century religion has been on the rise almost everywhere except Western Europe, where its decline continues. So the exception is Europe, not the United States. In Europe religion has been bound up with class and social conflict, and with centuries of bigotry and slaughter. Equivalent disasters have not disfigured America's religious inheritance. No one in America ever threatened to hang the last aristocrat with the entrails of the last priest, as they promised to do in the French Revolution. But then the French speak to this day of *l'exception francaise.*

The truth is that Europe and America are exceptional in different ways. To many America's religious behaviour seems exceptional in relation to America herself. She is the most modern nation on earth, and modernity is associated with Enlightenment secularism, science and representative government. So the question is: how can the democratically elected leader of a nation with the capacity to send men and women into space think that there is somebody up there who appointed him president at America's providential hour?

All American Presidents have been Christians, even if the faith of some has been stronger than of others. Indeed, as Samuel Huntington has noted, Americans tend to give to their country many of the attributes and functions of a church.[2] (The trouble arises when the same thing happens in reverse, as the churches attempt to speak for the country.) For all the constitutional separation between faith and state, America has never wholly accepted that religion is a private matter. The sheer size and presence of the churches make it hard to regard them as a subaltern part of American life. Whatever we think of their irruption into politics, there can be no denying their vitality, confidence and popular appeal, which contrast so startlingly with the embarrassed, compromising and defeatist tendencies of, for example, Anglicanism.

Had the growth of evangelism been no more than a response to 9/11 it could be written off as a natural reflex. An act of war against the American homeland, which not even Hitler managed, by a terrifying new breed of religious fascists might well have triggered, amongst other things, a religious response. Yet the influence of religion on American politics and society had been on the rise well before 9/11. The current phase began not with fundamentalist conservatives but with Jimmy Carter, the Southern Baptist and former Sunday school teacher, who proclaimed himself as 'born-again' in 1976. It was then that religion was given an office, as it were, in the White House. In 1978 the liberal *Evangelicals for Social Action* was founded. Simultaneously the Christian Right, with its worries about the teaching of more sex and less religion in schools and what they saw as other examples of post-Sixties decline, was on the rise. It is that that led to the Moral Majority.

Carter's domestic liberalism disappointed his Christian constituency, and his 'peace-through-compromise' foreign policy came to grief. President Reagan recruited evangelical support, but he too failed to satisfy his Christian electorate, championing family values more by his actorly rhetoric than by legislation. George Bush came across as uncomfortable with religion, though he too made gestures to the evangelicals, notably on abortion. With his Baptist, Bible belt background, Clinton played effectively to the liberal church. The way things were going made it natural that Al Gore, the opponent of George W. Bush in 2,000, should have discovered himself to be a born-again Christian half way through the election.

*

All this is unthinkable in Europe, where secularization continues apace. An average of 20% go regularly to a service, less than half the American figure, and in Eastern Europe only 14%. For all the realization that religion was more rooted in America, and despite stories in the press about credulous celebrities subscribing to this or that extravagant creed, the assumption was that America was moving in the same direction. For a brief moment it appeared that it was, but slight signs of a tailing off in religious commitment in the Seventies were soon reversed.

The biggest contrast is with the United Kingdom—paradoxically the closest parallel to America in terms of its Protestant inheritance. Britain is an increasingly irreligious society, with a steady decline in church-going amongst Catholics and Protestants alike. The mood of the times is revealed by the fact that an atheistic children's book, *His Dark Materials* by Philip Pullman, has been a best-seller with grown-ups, most of whom have never read the Bible but who increasingly read children's literature. Pullman's work, which was made into a successful play, drew admiring appreciations from predominantly non-religious reviewers and intellectuals. It is a safe bet that in America it will be outsold by the *Left Behind* series.

In Britain the Church becomes newsworthy only when sex or Royalty are involved, preferably the two together, such as the debate about whether or not the Archbishop of Canterbury should have smiled on the marriage of Prince Charles and his long-time partner in sin, Camilla. Though the Church seeks to involve itself in politics its interventions are of a generalized, 'do gooding' nature and their resonance close to zero. The fortunes of the Church of England in particular are at a low ebb. Its failure to resolve its own internal problems, notably over homosexuality, which threaten to bring about a schism in the Anglican community, further reduces the authority of its stance on political issues. There is a strong case for the Anglican church to be disestablished, but its lack of authority is such that most people do not care much one way or the other. The truth is that Anglicanism has already disestablished itself from their lives. In Britain the only sense in which politics and religion are coming together is in their joint decline. In 1979 the percentage of those attending church was 11.7%. Two decades later it was down to 7.5%. In the 1979 election some 70% of electors voted; in 2005 it was close to 60%.

Americans may not realize the extent to which politicians with strong beliefs like Tony Blair are an anomaly in national terms. The fact that the Prime Minister made almost no attempt to play on his Christianity in the recent election campaign is a token of the status of religion in Britain: it is difficult to imagine a White House spokesman saying, as Blair's former spokesman Alistair Campbell did, 'We don't do God'. His churchgoing is tolerated as a harmless eccentricity, but commentators are on the watch: one step too far and he would find himself caricatured as a Holy Joe. Asked on television whether he had prayed with George Bush on one of his trips to Washington, Blair declined to answer. There is no reason why he should not pray where and when he chooses, yet the question was designed to make him look foolish in British eyes, and he was wise not to reply. The incident tells us everything about the status of religion in contemporary Britain, and about how the religious revival in the United States is seen through British eyes.

In France, where only 52% believe in God, secularism in public affairs is a tenaciously upheld principle of the republic. The principle is especially strong in public education. The ban on Muslim girls from wearing headscarves to school two years ago, along with religious insignia of other faiths, was endorsed by all political parties, a large majority of the population, and not a few Muslim women. Even in strongly Catholic countries like Spain or Italy the high standing of religion is not quite what it seems. Formally the church remains vigorous, and grieving over the death of the Pope was a mass event. Yet its authority is in decline. While belief remains the norm, reluctance to heed the Vatican's advice on birth control— a key element of its teaching—has led to an extraordinary fall in birth rates in both countries. Pride in their countries' Christian traditions, a secular critic might observe, does not translate into a determination to produce more Christians.

*

Chief amongst the worries of the American religious Right is their country's godless hedonism. Would a return to the principles of fundamentalist religion, enacted in law, moderate America's lusts? Instantly the conflict between individual rights and social control is raised. Coercive legislation is not an option, because it would fly in the face of the country's most basic principles. The religious traditions the conservatives want to invoke are also a primary source of American freedoms, and when personal liberties are at stake what has been given cannot easily be taken away.

The ideal of the Christian Right is presumably a return to the pre-Kinsey society of the 1950s, perceived as a time of God-fearing family life, sexual moderation, and innocent popular songs like Frank Weir's *The Happy Wanderer* or the Gaylords' *Little Shoemaker.* Let us leave aside the question of whether those halcyon days ever truly existed (though unfortunately those excruciating lyrics did.) A deeper, and simpler question must be asked. For all its alleged depravity America remains the most religious country in the Western world. In a nation where a large majority describe themselves as believers, and almost 50% are churchgoers, one might reasonably expect a level of public morality far higher than elsewhere. A glance at American society is enough to show that this is not the case. If the evangelical movement succeeds in converting the godless, the result will be an even higher percentage of self-described Christians, or of born-again believers. Whether that would suffice to make America a more godly society is open to question. It would certainly make it a more hypocritical one.

The statement that America is a highly religious society is of course comparative. In historical terms it tells us little, since faith today is a far cry from faith as understood by Americans in the distant past. To have put to them the question that is put by today's pollsters— 'How central is religion to your daily life?'—would have made no sense whatever: religion *was* their lives. So was a permanent consciousness of sin, fear of retribution, and a terror of damnation. Now that God has become a more friendly, approachable fellow such terms are largely metaphors, incantations that have lost their sting. 60% of Americans may say they believe in hell but they do not expect to be roasted alive when they die if they under-declare their income to the IRS, or conduct an adulterous liaison.

Religious belief in the twenty-first century is of a

different order. At best it entails a genuine humility before God, accompanied by an attempt to live an honest, useful, socially engaged life. At worst it is a shallow, self-regarding thing, a form of spiritual narcissism whose practice involves few duties, little self-sacrifice, and a good deal of pious pretence. Either way contemporary religion is submerged in the materialism of the age. That alone makes it a less authoritative source of moral values.

There are Americans who insist that foreigners have got the evangelical thing out of proportion.[3] According to this view religion is only one aspect of a richer American culture. Revivalists are not at war with the contemporary world, and being born-again is a new way of becoming involved in modernity. Far from being dour, backward-looking and forbidding, the evangelical movement is upbeat, with forms of worship that are populist, joyous and colourful. And though most pay lip service to scriptural infallibility by no means all those involved could be described as fundamentalists, the emphasis being less on theological rectitude than on 'feel-good' religion.

Its contemporary nature (the argument goes on) is reflected in the fact that many of those involved are women with quasi-feminist attitudes, who feel drawn to 'lifestyle evangelism.' Hence books like *The Total Woman,* by an evangelical Christian, Marabel Morgan, who told women that orgasms were not an occasional gift from men, but an entitlement. Or *Slim for Him,* which tells them they are doing God's work in the world by shedding weight, and that lightness would get its reward in heaven. Or there is *Revolve*, a girls' magazine that serializes the Bible in pictorial, teenage form, and pop religious music.

This analysis is comforting, but presents problems. The happy-clappy element in the evangelical movement certainly makes it difficult to sustain the claim that the USA is on its way to becoming a fully-fledged theocracy. But except amongst America's more extreme critics, that was never the apprehension. The fear was of religion exercising an undue influence on American politics, and importing anti-rational factors into the national debate, not only on abortion or gay issues but on foreign policy.

In any event the idea that fundamentalism is less fundamental than it appears is not necessarily consoling. The suggestion is that what we are seeing is religiosity rather than religion, coupled with a social agenda: in other words a kind of mass therapy with a political edge. Suppose that is true. How would it help America, in the words of John Adams, to be 'sprinkled all over with false converts'? The question arises: which is worse? A church that infuses politics with dated dogma, or a spontaneous, unthinking, self-indulgent, infantile approach to religious faith? Both would be bad news for democracy. People in a state of spiritual stimulation are more easily manipulated by pietized politicians, and by weakening the power of reason in the social and political process their delusions can do themselves, and their country, great damage.

Populist forms of faith are not new, and the precedents are not encouraging. In the Great Awakening of the early eighteenth century the Reverend George Whitfield enthralled the bumpkins of Georgia with his pulpit caperings. Congregations ran amok, or rolled screaming on the floor. Then there was Charles Finney, an evangelist in the 1820s, who used humorous routines to recruit new souls. Calvinism had always been distrustful of emotion, and such outbreaks can be seen as another reaction against the Puritan tradition. The suspicion must be that something different—and arguably worse—is at work today. Evangelism is in theory a response to a soulless, self-centred, materialist civilization. Yet the forms of worship it frequently adopts are based on sentimentality, a smarmy 'sincerity', and 'me-first' emotionalism, rather than disciplined thought or sacrifice. (The growth of informal religion is not confined to America, or to Protestantism. At the funeral of Pope John in Rome in April 2005 many of the public mourners queuing to see his body lie in state were clapping and laughing in a way which would never have happened in the past.)

The swing from feel-bad to feel-good forms of worship that we are witnessing can take troubling forms. The kind of revivalism that comes from the same stable of emotions as Diana-worship in Britain, or manifests itself in a half-crazed addiction to dieting, has little to do with religion in the most responsible sense—and religion is nothing if it is not responsible. What is certain is that showmanship increases the appeal of evangelism to the young, the poor, the inadequately educated, and to the hopelessly impressionable. 'Soft' forms of religious worship, moreover, appear to be compatible with hard-line attitudes. The result can be a noxious mixture of emotional religiosity and populist politics. 'A God-intoxicated country' America has been called, and a state of intoxication is not compatible with social and political sobriety.

Gertrude Himmelfarb, the conservative writer and academic, also questions the idea that America is awash with religious extremism. Evangelism, in her reading, is a misleading, catch-all phrase. Religious revivalists are fired up not only by same-sex marriage, stem-cell research and abortion. For many, including some non-believers, the significance of the movement lies in the rising discontent with levels of violence, pornography and the rest. What it showed was that there was a widespread feeling that the permissive society had gone too far and that it was time for a return to the kind of 'Victorian family values' promoted by Mrs Thatcher in Britain (with startling lack of success, it should be added.)

She is right that American evangelism has always been more socially and politically diverse than is understood in Europe. Its allies can include Jews and Catholics, not to speak of Muslims. Nor are African Americans, over-whelmingly evangelical, likely to identify with the Christian Right. But her claim that 'moral values derive more from tradition than from dogma, from the sense of family and community than from scripture or the church' underplays the extent to which American communities began under the aegis of authoritarian religious rule. Her suggestion that in America 'the moral sense is antecedent to religion' is especially unconvincing. American social mores are deeply influenced by Puritanical beliefs, and for Puritans religion and the moral sense were indivisible.

'We don't stop watching the trash on television' Himmelfarb concludes, 'but we elect a president who seems to speak for our better selves, for those moral values that we habitually violate.'[4] Like the claim that American revivalism is 'soft' rather than 'hard', and so nothing to worry about, this is unlikely to put minds at rest. The fact that the public vote for a god-fearing family man before turning back to the godless TV trash produced by corporations whose leaders no doubt voted for him as well, is the reverse of reassuring. On the contrary it illustrates a vein of hypocrisy, by no means confined to America, but one that is embedded deep in its Puritan traditions, to whose ideas of social control conservative evangelicals appear to seek to return.

Americans, it is said, have become a nation of seekers, frustrated spiritualists who are 'looking for something'. Surveying some of the forms religious revivalism takes makes it hard to believe they are looking very hard. Certainly it does not suggest that they are prepared to renounce material comforts, or to pursue more demanding forms of spiritual engagement. Along with an undoubted concern about values, might not this seeking reflect little more than a modern form of anomie, accompanied by vague stirrings of the soul? A feeling of boredom and satiety and a need for distraction?

To judge by statistics America appears to take religion seriously, but she seems less serious about the form that religion takes. The success of the *Left Behind* series of books (more than fifty million copies sold since 1995), or of Dan Brown's mystical absurdity *The Da Vinci Code*, suggests that the answer is: not very. Books of this kind can be seen as entertainment or harmless nonsense. One thing they are not is a sign of profound religious feeling. Their success owes more to escapism, credulity, sentimentality, infantilisation and poor literary taste—things that any self-respecting evangelical concerned with the moral health of society would deplore.

Such phenomena are evidence less of a new spirituality than of religion gone to seed. Certainly there is little comparison between today's vapourisings and the Puritan search for an accommodation between man's religious and social natures.

'The toleration of all religions and persuasions' Increase Mather inveighed 'is the way to have no true religion left.'[5] This may seem little more than a typically intolerant remark, but in contemporary terms it could be on the nail. The fragmentation of the American church into myriad denominations, millennial sects and personalized creeds adds to the impression that what we are seeing is not a rebirth of faith but a sprawl of spiritual self-indulgence. A dizzying plurality of churches (there are over three hundred types of Baptists alone) disperses influence, and could prove a check to religion's political clout. The Latino community, which has grown 150% since 1980, surpassing the black population, no longer represents a solid Catholic segment. Catholicism is losing members to less traditional Protestant churches, especially the Pentacostals, and Southern Baptists are unhappy about the progress made by charismatics and the rest. Shifts of allegiance are accompanied by tension between churches on political and social issues, and conflicting views exist amongst evangelicals, notably on abortion.

Americans talk of the religious marketplace. The analogy is apt, if unflattering, increasing the impression that the new spiritualism is infected with the excess of worldliness it condemns. Wesley's words are yet again apposite. 'I fear, wherever riches have increased, the essence of religion has decreased in the same proportion.

271

Therefore I do not see how it is possible, in the nature of things, for any revival of true religion to continue long.' The operative words are 'true religion'. How much true religion is involved where churches tempt customers through advertising, the hard sell and spiritual and monetary bribery, and where non-Catholic denominations poach Latino members by dangling the bait of services in Spanish and aid to Latino communities?

Like department stores that have failed to move with the times and are destined to be overtaken by bigger, flashier and more welcoming malls, or by specialized style-conscious boutiques, mainline churches are losing out. In 1960 over 40% of white adults were members of mainline denominations, and only 27% affiliated to evangelical churches. Now they are level-pegging, with the mainline churches tending down. Currently Catholics retain some 25% of 'the market', though with its paedophile scandals and the death of a charismatic Pope, there are fears for its future. Attendance rates at Mass are down, as is compliance with official doctrine: the rigorous approach to birth control and abortion preached by the Vatican are not reflected in the personal lives of a large number of Catholics.

For obvious reasons the tide is running against churches with liturgies and organ music and sober-faced ministers, in favour of denominations with more contem-porary styles, including lusty singing by good-looking girls or boys, in whose mouths songs about godly love take on pleasing ambiguities. The Pentacostals, the most successful in this line of worship and the fastest growing church, are keener on spiritual feeling than on doctrine, an emphasis clearly congenial to the mood of the times. Their contemporary, business-like ethos is reflected in their revival of church tithes.

Religious consumerism has overtones of fashion, and fashion is the opposite of eternal values. The sleeker and glossier the product, and the less it demands in terms of care and maintenance, the more attractive it will be. The fact that a church or chapel offering popular songs and a simple religious message will out-sell one with a wheezing organ and an over-cerebral theology is unsurprising; nor is it something, one would have thought, that would hearten the defenders of religion.

*

'They dealt with the degenerate times by reviving the old Puritan concern with the conviction of sin, the necessity of conversion and the certainty of salvation. Spectacular results were achieved...but, as in all such cases, a few years later the effects had largely worn off and the good people of Boston and Philadelphia felt free to dance again.'[6]

So wrote the English historian of America Hugh Brogan about the Presbyterian revivalists of the early nineteen hundreds. In a world where singing and dancing can form part of evangelism's attractions, how long will the current upsurge of religiosity endure? Where fashion and emotion play so large a part it is impossible to be sure. Revivalism could blow itself out quickly, and leave little in its wake. Though if Samuel Huntington is right, and what we are seeing is a reassertion of the Protestant understanding of the American way of life, it could last longer. A feeling that this way of living has been hollowed out by permissiveness and immigration, together with an Islamic fundamentalist threat from abroad, could keep religion in the forefront of the country's agenda. Another reason analysts of evangelism are convinced it will endure is that, as two Republican presidential victories have shown, politically, it works.

For the moment. Like President Carter, Bush could find that it is one thing to have born-again principles, another to apply them in the real world. And even if it lasts a decade revivalism could prove to be little more than an ephemeral phase in America's history. Rich countries, like rich people, get bored. The media tire of things, and it may be that after a year or two evangelism will cease to be a story. Public moods are increasingly volatile and there seems no reason why religion should not suffer as much as everything else from a chronically low attention span. There is certainly little sign that America as a whole is prepared to sacrifice the comforts of its lifestyle and embark on a long-term course of national redemption: to become, as it were, a born-again country.

Nor should reactions against the new religiosity be underrated. Religious liberty includes liberty from religion. If the influence of evangelicals can seem out of proportion to their number, the same can be said of the non-believing. Alongside the political-religious nexus a parallel, secularizing world exists—in the media, the civil service, science, schools and universities—and Christian conservative attempts to infiltrate it will be resisted. Here and there they may seem to be on the retreat, but educational and government bureaucracies are powerful things, well schooled in the art of absorbing outside influences the better to dilute them.

Within the Republican Party itself, stresses are developing. The traditional overlap between believers and right-wing voters is one thing, mixing politics and religion another. 'Can anyone look at the carnage in Iran, the bloodshed in Northern Ireland or the bombs bursting in Lebanon and yet question the dangers of injecting religious issues into the affairs of state?' warned the arch-conservative Barry Goldwater decades ago.[7] Will the Republican Party succeed in making use of the men of faith, as President Nixon did with Billy Graham, for his own purposes, or could it be the other way round? Signs that the GOP's Christian affiliations could become a divisive force are mounting. A tougher breed of religious activist has come to the fore, and already some Republicans are warning that the party is being transformed into the political arm of Conservative Christians. Similar stresses could develop amongst the Democrats, where liberal evangelicals accuse the party's secular tendency of consigning it to permanent opposition by failing to respond to the left-of-centre religious vote. And even if the Democrats succeed in heightening the Party's appeal to churchgoers, the religious factions on both sides of the political line could cancel one another out.

Then there is the commercial interest, whose ties with the GOP bring them into alignment, voluntary or otherwise, with the evangelicals. With business on a looser rein than ever before, and the evangelicals on a tighter one, a more frequent collision of interests seems guaranteed. The business of business is profits, the business of the churches are ethics. The evangelicals are more worried about morality than the economy; with business it is the other way round. Evangelists want to open people's eyes to their sinful habits; in sex, food, entertainment or consumerism, business wants to exploit them. Some evangelicals are catching on to environmental issues, in the interests of preserving God's creation. Business interests are concerned with preserving margins. In foreign affairs evangelicals are concerned by the absence of human rights, notably the right to worship; commerce seeks international markets, and has more earthly priorities. If there were tensions between the commercial and religious interests in seventeenth century America there most certainly will be now.

Politics, business and religion are potentially hostile partners. In the end social censoriousness is irreconcilable, as the Puritans found, with economic liberalism. Conservative fundamentalists believe in freedom of enterprise but not of sexuality. For right-wing libertarians, choice and diversity are key. For liberals choice applies more to social than to economic questions. To complicate things further liberal-minded Protestants can have more in common with so-called secular elites than they have with their co-religionaries of a more conservative stamp.

If business and evangelism are unnatural bedmates, points of contact between black and white evangelicals are even harder to perceive. African-Americans are over-whelmingly Protestant and evangelical, but cultural and political attitudes mean they have little in common with

Christian fundamentalists. So while they can be conservative on abortion, they can be more tolerant about gays. And unlike their white conservative counterparts they favour more government spending to improve the lot of their communities.

*

Concerns about values are no monopoly of religious zealots. Nor are attempts to find solutions. The problems are real, but their dramatization can be artificial. The habit of inflating shades of opinion into full-blown conflicts of principle is another aspect of America's search for absolutes. But reality has a way of reasserting itself; it did so for the Puritans and it will do so now. The fact that religion in America has tended to stress the need for engagement with the world makes religious feelings more subject to influence by temporal factors. The more conservative-minded evangelicals enter into politics the more likely they are, like the Puritans before them, to overreach themselves and be forced into accommodations. And if politicians like President Bush make promises which public sentiment or the law of the land prevent them from fulfilling, as happened in the recent right-to-life case involving Terri Schiavo, disillusionment could follow. The event was a reminder of what many Americans instinctively know: that a secular approach is the only basis on which modern governments and a civil society can operate.

Secular representative government in America grew out of the English reformation, the American Revolution, the Enlightenment, and two centuries of struggle for democratic values at home and abroad. The idea that the world's richest, most scientifically and technologically advanced democracy should regress to a state of atavistic religiosity is surreal. Perhaps what we are witnessing is the opposite of what we are encouraged to believe: not a strengthening but a weakening of America's religious traditions, under the strain of the conflicts they contain.

Contemplating the fact that the Lakewood church, the first in the United States to average more than 30,000 worshippers a week, has moved into a sports stadium to accommodate its congregation, what are we to think? There is no cross or altar, but a giant TV and video game booths. Music and a light show feature, and its telegenic pastor, Joel Osteen, greets the crowd with words suggestive of a pop lyric: 'I just want to say that I love you.' Is this born-again America—or evidence of America's dwindling religious faith? Is the clamour of the congregation the hallelujah of a freshly converted people? Or is it what Matthew Arnold called in his poem Dover Beach, lamenting the triumph of materialism in nineteenth century Britain, religion's 'melancholy, long withdrawing roar'?

Appropriately, the Lakewood church's home is in Texas. Which prompts the thought that revivalism could reach its zenith under President Bush and be destined for decline. Mainline churches could dissolve first into fundamentalism, then a New Age spiritualism, and thence into a kind of civil religion with a populist political slant. For all the sanctimonious self-indulgence that may have to be endured while the process works through, such an outcome could have attractions. For one thing it would be an improvement on what has happened in Britain. There the decline of religion has left a spiritual and social vacuum, not least in working class areas. Where the church or chapel once acted as a social adhesive, now there is little or nothing left. Deconsecrated chapels are transformed into flats, and drug-takers gather in abandoned churchyards. For America this seems an improbable future. Churches there will always be. Imagining America without religion is like imagining Britain without class.

America is the world's greatest democracy, and as such owes the world an example. Her problems, domestic or international, must be resolved by elected politicians rather than by Biblical exegesis, no matter whose bible it is. In Europe culture wars are pursued by secular institutions reacting to popular concern rather than to religious pressure. In America too individuals, the law, pressure groups, business and political movements can negotiate solutions to conflicts between public morality and personal choice, with an input from the church.

The issues are less clear-cut than they are presented and the scope for compromise is there. Abortion in America remains amongst the most liberal in the world, and it is not impossible to envisage a cross-party consensus for agreed limits. Similarly it is not unthinkable for America to become a country where civil unions for homosexuals rather than marriage become tolerated by the majority, where gun ownership and pornography are more tightly controlled, or where environmentalism becomes a new priority. Nor is it inconceivable to think of America reverting, under the pressure of its own and international opinion, to a less confrontational approach to the world.

*

For Tawny, what characterized America's preeminent religion was its tension.

'The Puritan is like a steel spring, compressed by an inner force, which shatters every obstacle by its rebound. Sometimes the strain is too tense, and, when its imprisoned energy is released, it shatters itself.'[8]

William James, in *Varieties of Religious Experience*, appeared to hold out the prospect of relief: 'The transition from tenseness, self-responsibility, and worry, to equanimity, receptivity and peace is the most wonderful of all the shiftings of inner equilibrium.' Is America shattering itself? Or can she regain some inner equilibrium? If ever a country needed a release from tension it is the United States today. It is impossible to live at the current pitch, and yet a shattered America seems beyond imagination. Talk of the country subsiding into economic crisis and a fascistic regime, or of an empire over-reaching itself and destined for a fall, smack of imported European notions of decline. As many have noted, debate about declinism in America reached a peak in the Eighties, the very moment of a new surge of energy and prosperity, and the empire that collapsed was not America's but Russia's.

Andrew Delbanco has spoken of his country's 'unslaked craving for transcendence.'[9] Faith will persist, because faith is engrained in the country's history—what

280

Cotton Mather called Theopolis Americana. In fact America's spiritual temperament is so fulsome that it overflows, revealing itself in the most unlikely places. Examples can be found in three major thinkers who hold no brief for established churches—Daniel Bell, Michael Walzer and John Rawls. Bell believes that religious creeds are not erased by the development of a rational consciousness, if only because they continue to offer an explanation of the absurdities of life, such as death itself, and at the very least provide comfort. In seeking to describe the American ethos, even this clear-eyed sociologist can have recourse to religious terminology:

'One senses, in reflecting on American political development, that there was something *exceptional* about the nation's history and character, exceptional not necessarily in the sense of being exempt from some presumed laws of social evolution, but as providing, in the theological and political nuances of the term, *a saving grace* which makes us still exemplary for other nations.'[10]

Michael Walzer appears to echo Bell's view when he suggests that the harsher sides of Puritanism can be separated from its more benign aspects, and that a sense of America's spiritual destiny is no monopoly of the political Right:

'In a sense, it might be said that liberalism is dependent upon the existence of saints—that is, of men whose good behaviour can be relied on. At the same time, the secular and genteel character of liberalism is determined by the fact that these are men whose goodness (sociability, self-discipline, moral decency, or mere respectability) is self-assured and relaxed, entirely free from the nerviness and fanaticism of Calvinist godliness.'[11]

When John Rawls, philosopher and author of the influential *A Theory of Justice*, died in January 2003, the following quotation from his work was reproduced in the *New York Review of Books*.[12] Entitled *In Memoriam* it was signed, appropriately, by the Harvard University Press, itself an indirect product of the Puritan era:

The perspective of eternity is not a perspective from a certain place beyond the world, not the point of view of a transcendent being; rather it is a certain form of thought and feeling that rational persons can adopt within the world. And having done so, they can, whatever their generation, bring together into one scheme all individual perspectives and arrive at regulative principles that can be affirmed by everyone as he lives by them, each from his own standpoint. Purity of heart, if one could attain it, would be to see clearly and to act with grace and self-command from this point of view.

It is a flavourful passage. Rawls is careful to emphasize the secular nature of his thoughts, and the divines of New England would have been too horrified to notice that it is drenched in Puritan sentiment and imagery. The fact that in the flesh the philosopher had a sacerdotal manner makes it the more suggestive, and Rawls lays out his credo in the tones of a seventeenth-century preacher. What he is saying is that given the right thoughts and feelings, with grace and self-command and purity of heart—all of them Puritan concepts—a form of eternity is available, by which man might yet be saved.

The Puritan tradition may be in crisis, but in America even rationalism and secularism, it seems, are suffused with faith. Which in a rational world ought to make accommodation between believers and non-believers easier.

AFTERWORD

As a British diplomat in Paris in the late seventies I had a strange conversation with a French Communist leader (the Communists were in alliance with the Socialists at the time.) We were discussing events in Britain and my communist was a worried man. At the time Britain was in a state of chaos: the Labour Government was divided, the economy was in trouble, and the trade unions rampant to the point where wildcat strikes were the norm. A low point had been reached shortly before our conversation: not only was the rubbish piling up in the streets but, due to a strike by grave-diggers, the dead were left unburied.

This was the scenario that was to lead to the election of Mrs Thatcher, but that was not the Frenchman's chief concern. Except when they are directing it Communists have a horror of disorder. Far from indicating solidarity with his trade union brothers, with an air of incredulity mixed with indignation the Frenchman asked me what the hell was going on? To him it looked as if civil society in Britain was falling apart. Did I realize the gravity of that for the Continent, who throughout their wars and upheavals had always looked to the British as a point of stability? I took my lesson from the Communist with due humility.

At their least prejudiced and most reflective European feelings about America today have something of the Frenchman's attitude towards Britain. Beneath all the ridicule, resentment, snobbery and covert envy with which America is regarded, and the pretence that a united Europe would be better off without her, her problems are seen with an underlying sense of foreboding. It is not simply a matter of her economic importance to Europe and the world. Nor is it a question of the security of the West, fundamental as that is. It is a feeling that America, 'brash', 'overbearing' and 'fanatical' though she is, continues to represent all that in innovative and dynamic, a homeland not just of liberty but of contemporary civilization.

What message would it send to the new societies of China, Russia and Eastern Europe, not to speak of the still more fragile democratic forces in the Middle East, if America were perceived to be subsiding into a mood of rancour, defeat and introversion? Who would replace her? Certainly not Europe, which as recent events have shown remains spectacularly fragmented. A European foreign policy is a beautiful dream or a bureaucratic nightmare; either way it remains an abstraction. Definitely not the United Nations, vital as it is. Any international organization can only work with the material at its disposal, and with a high percentage of its membership consisting of non-democratic regimes, authoritarian states or out-and-out dictatorships, its efficiency and integrity, let alone its moral authority, seem likely to remain in doubt. The idea of Russia and China extending their international power to fill the gap left by an America in decline, besides being a tragic historical irony, would be an awesome prospect.

All these are reasons for regarding America's national and international travails with concern rather than with satisfaction. For those who do, watching America's President perform in public ceases to be an occasion for hilarity and becomes an ordeal. The problem is not simply his uncertain command of English; people didn't feel embarrassed by Eisenhower. Nor is it his populist style; the sight of a President in confident touch with his people can be reassuring. The explanation of our trepidation is simpler and deeper. The ordeal springs from the fear that America's duly elected president and *de facto* leader of the Western world might at any moment do or say something foolish and undignified: smirk, swagger, or have resort to some maudlin pietism. Anti-Americans relish these moments; those who believe that the world would be a much worse place without America's power and influence do not. Our pain comes from the knowledge that he is demeaning his nation in the eyes of the world, and that a majority of America's electors do not seem to understand it.

The spectacle of America at prayer may dismay and disorientate the world, but there are reasons to pray for America.

SELECT BIBLIOGRAPHY

David Aikman, *A Man of Faith, The Spiritual Journey of George W,
Bush*, W Publishing Group, Nashville, 2004

Bernard Bailyn, *The Origins of American Politics*, Vintage Books, New
York 1970

Andrew Barr, *Drink, A Social History of America*, Carroll and Graf, New
York, 1999

Daniel J, Boorstin, *The Americans*, Vintage Books, New York, 1958
―――――――――, *Hidden History*, Vintage Books, New York 1989

Hugh Brogan, *The Penguin History of the USA*, London 1999

Bruce C, Daniels, *Puritans at Play*, St Martins' Griffin, New York, 1995

Andrew Delbanco, *The Puritan Ordeal*, Harvard University Press, 1989
―――――――――, *The Real American Dream*, Harvard University Press,
1999

Christopher Durston, *The Culture of English Puritanism 1560-1700*,
Macmillan, London, 1996

Niall Ferguson, 'Economics, Religion, and the Decline of Europe',
Economic Affairs, Vol. 24, issue 4, December 2004

Stephen Foster, *The Long Argument, 1570-1700*, University of North
Carolina, 1991

Robert Fowler, *Religion and Politics in America*, Westview Press,
Boulder Colorado, 2004

Christopher Hill, *Puritanism and Revolution*, Panther, London, 1968

————————, *Reformation to Industrial Revolution*, Pelican, London, 1969

Samuel Huntington, *Who Are We?*, Simon and Schuster, London 2004

Edmund Leites, *The Puritan Conscience and Modern Sexuality*, Yale University Press, 1986

Seymour Martin Lipsett, *It Didn't Happen Here*, Norton, New York, 2000

Stephen Mansfield, *The Faith of George W. Bush*, Penguin, New York, 2004

N.S., McFetridge, *Calvinism in History*, Still Waters Revival Books, Edmonton, 1989

Perry Miller, *The New England Mind*, Harvard University Press, 1939

Edmund S, Morgan, *The Puritan Family*, Harper Torchbacks, New York 1966

Michael Novak, *Business as a Calling*, The Free Press, New York 1996

Camille Paglia, *Sex, Art and American Culture*, Viking, London 1993

Octavio Paz, *Covergences, Essays on Art and Literature*, Bloomsbury, London 1987

Philippe Roger, *The American Enemy*, University of Chicago Press, 2005

George Santayana, *Santayana on America*, Lyon, New York 1968

Lawrence A. Sasek, *Images of English Puritanism, A Collection of Contemporary Sources, 1589-1646*, Louisiana State University Press, 1989

Franny Schaeffer, *Is Capitalism Christian?* Crossway Books, Westchester Illinois, 1985

Lawrence Stone, *The Family, Sex and Marriage in England, 1500-1800*, Weidenfeld and Nicholson, London 1977

R.H., Tawney, *Religion and the Rise of Capitalism*, Pelican, 1964

Jim Wallis, *God's Politics*, Picador, London 2001

Max Weber, *The Protestant Ethic and the Spirit of Capitalism*, Routledge, London 1992

Tom Wolfe, *Hooking Up*, Picador, London 2001

————————, *The Right Stuff, Farrar*, Strauss Giroux, New York 1979

NOTES

INTRODUCTION

1   Perry Miller, *The New England Mind*
2   Robert Fowler, *Religion and Politics in America*
3   Stephen Foster, *The Long Argument, 1570-1700*

CHAPTER ONE

1   George Santayana, *Santayana on America*
2   Christopher Hill, *Puritanism and Revolution*
3   Perry Miller, *The New England Mind*
4   R.H. Tawney, *Religion and the Rise of Capitalism*
5   Samuel Huntington, *Who Are We?*
6   Michael Lind, *Prospect*, November 2001

CHAPTER TWO

1   Perry Miller, *The New England Mind*
2   *Ibid*
3   Andrew Barr, *Drink, A Social History of America*

4   *Ibid*

5   Octavio Paz, *Convergences, Essays on Art and Literature*

6   *Sartor Resartus*, Thomas Carlyle

7   Perry Miller, *The New England Mind*

8   *Ernest Hemingway on Writing*, Grafton Books, London, 1985

9   Daniel J, Boorstin, *Hidden History*

10   Perry Miller, *The New England Mind*

11   *Scott Fitzgerald Letters*

12   Max Weber, *The Protestant Ethic and the Spirit of Capitalism*

13   Andrew Delbanco, *The Real American Dream*

14   Nietzsche, Friedrich, *Why I Am So Wise*, Penguin, 2004

15   *The Economist*, 5 March 2005

16   *The Puritans*, New York, 1938

17   *Ibid*

18   Perry Miller, *The New England Mind*

19   H.L. Mencken

20   Selected from *The New York Review of Books*, 7 April 2005

21   *Approaching Artaud, Under the Sign of Saturn*, Vintage 2001

22   Perry Miller, *The New England Mind*

23   *Ibid*

24   *Ibid*

25   *Ibid*

26   *Ibid*

27   Lawrence Stone, *The Family, Sex and Marriage in England, 1500-1800*

28   Perry Miller, *The New England Mind*

CHAPTER THREE

1   *The Times*, 15 May 2001

2   Edmund S, Morgan, *The Puritan Family*

3   Edmund Leites, *The Puritan Conscience and Modern Sexuality*

4   *Ibid*

5   *Ibid,*

6   *Ibid*

7   Edmund S, Morgan, *The Puritan Family*

8   *Ibid*

9   Perry Miller, *The New England Mind*

10   Edmund Leites, *The Puritan Conscience and Modern Sexuality*

11   Lawrence Stone, *The Family, Sex and Marriage in England, 1500-1800*

12   Robert Fowler, *Religion and Politics in America*

13   Philippe Roger, *The American Enemy*

14   Perry Miller, *The New England Mind*

15   Camille Paglia, *Sex, Art and American Culture*

16   *Ibid*

17   *The Sunday Telegraph Magazine*, 19 June 2005

18   Barbey d'Aurevilly, *Le Dandysme et George Brummell*, Gibson Square, London, 2002

19   Perry Miller, *The New England Mind*

20   *Ibid*

21   Edmund S, Morgan, *The Puritan Family*

22   *Ibid*

23   Baudelaire, *Intimate Journals*

24   Perry Miller, *The New England Mind*

25   John Updike, *The Early Stories*, Hamish Hamilton, 2004

CHAPTER FOUR

1   Macaulay, *The Economic Consequences of the Revolution*

2   Perry Miller, *The New England Mind*

3   Michael Walzer, *Puritanism as a Revolutionary Ideology, History and Theory*, Vol 3, 1963

4   R.H. Tawney, *Religion and the Rise of Capitalism*

5   Perry Miller, *The New England Mind*

6   *Ibid*

7   *Ibid*

8   R.H. Tawney, *Religion and the Rise of Capitalism*, in *The Tradesman's Calling*

9   Perry Miller, *The New England Mind*

10   Robert Southey, *The Life of Wesley*, c1820

11   Michael Novak, *Business as a Calling*

12   London School of Economics, for the Sutton Trust

13   Jeffrey Sachs, *The End of Poverty*, Allen Lane, London 2005

NOTES

14   *Economic Affairs*, volume 24, issue 4 page 37

15   Perry Miller, *The New England Mind*

16   *Ibid*

17   *Ibid*

18   *Ibid*

19   Max Weber, *The Protestant Ethic and the Spirit of Capitalism*

20   *Ibid*

21   *Ibid*

22   Stephen K. McDowell, *America's Providential History,* Providence Foundation, 1989

23   American Enterprise Institute Conference on *'Capitalism and Socialism, a Theological Enquiry'*

24   Perry Miller, *The New England Mind*

25   Christopher Hill, *Puritanism and Revolution*

26   Richard P. McCormick, *The Origin of American Politics*

27   Perry Miller, *The New England Mind*

28   *Ibid*

29   *New York Magazine*, August 18, 1986

30   The Treaty of Tripoli

31   Stephen Mansfield, *The Faith of George W, Bush,* Penguin, 2003

32   Perry Miller, *The New England Mind*

33   George W. Bush, *A Charge to Keep, The Campaign Biography*, William Morrow 1999

34   *The Times*, 21 February 2005

35   Jim Wallis, *God's Politics*

CHAPTER SIX

1   Sarah Walden, *Whistler and his Mother, an Unexpected Relationship*, Gibson Square Books, 2001

2   Bad News, *Observer,* 10 April 2005

3   *The Times*, 5 March 2005

4   Johann Gottfried Herder *Outlines of a Philosophy of the History of Man*

5   Perry Miller, *The New England Mind*

6   Speech by Henry Kissinger

7   Philippe Roger, *The American Enemy*

NOTES

CHAPTER SEVEN

1. Alain Minc, *Ce Monde Qui Vient*, Grasset, 2004
2. *Independent*, 15 December 2001
3. Dr Yusuf al-Qaradawi, *The Times*, 16 July 2005
4. *The Downfall*, directed by Olivier Hirschbiegel
5. Baudrillard quoted in Philippe Roger, *The American Enemy*
6. Landscapes of the Jihad, Militancy, Morality and Modernity, *New York Review of Books*, 11 August 2005
7. George Santayana, *Santayana on America*

CHAPTER EIGHT

1. Andrew Greeley 'American Exceptionalism, The Religious Phenomenon' in *Is America Different? A New Look at American Exceptionalism*, ed. Byron Schafer, Oxford, 1991
2. Huntington, *American Politics*
3. Alan Wolfe, Dieting for Jesus, *Prospect* January 2004
4. Himmelfarb, *The Sunday Times*, 7 November, 2004
5. Perry Miller, *The New England Mind*
6. Hugh Brogan, *The Penguin History of the USA*, London 1999
7. Barry Goldwater
8. R.H. Tawney, *Religion and the Rise of Capitalism*
8. Andrew Delbanco, *The Real American Dream*, Harvard University Press, 1999
9. Daniel Bell, *American Exceptionalism*
10. Michael Walzer, *Puritanism as a Revolutionary Ideology, History and Theory*, Vol 3, 1963
11. *New York Review of Books*, 16 January 2005

INDEX

INDEX